The Bower Atmosphere

A BIOGRAPHY OF B. M. BOWER

VICTORIA LAMONT

University of Nebraska Press
Lincoln

The letter from B. M. Bower to Guy Weadick is reproduced courtesy of the Guy Weadick fonds of the Glenbow Library. The Bertrand Sinclair letters, 1958–1960 (Sinclair to Claude Dowen, 20 December 1959), SC 1349, are reproduced courtesy of the Montana Historical Society Research Center.

The University of Nebraska Press is part of a land-grant institution with campuses and programs on the past, present, and future homelands of the Pawnee, Ponca, Otoe-Missouria, Omaha, Dakota, Lakota, Kaw, Cheyenne, and Arapaho Peoples, as well as those of the relocated Ho-Chunk, Sac and Fox, and Iowa Peoples.

Publication of this volume was assisted by the University of Waterloo.

Library of Congress Cataloging-in-Publication Data
Names: Lamont, Victoria, author.
Title: The Bower atmosphere : a biography of B. M. Bower / Victoria Lamont.
Description: Lincoln : University of Nebraska Press, 2024. |
Includes bibliographical references and index.
Identifiers: LCCN 2023044399
ISBN 9781496236210 (paperback)
ISBN 9781496239068 (epub)
ISBN 9781496239075 (pdf)
Subjects: LCSH: Bower, B. M., 1871–1940 | Women authors, American—
Biography. | Authors, American—20th century—Biography. |
BISAC: BIOGRAPHY & AUTOBIOGRAPHY / Literary Figures |
BIOGRAPHY & AUTOBIOGRAPHY / Women
Classification: LCC PS3503.O8193 Z75 2024 | DDC 813/.52 [B]
—dc23/eng/20231012
LC record available at https://lccn.loc.gov/2023044399

Set in Minon Pro by K. Andresen

For Reed Doke
Thank you for trusting me with this story

CONTENTS

ILLUSTRATIONS

PREFACE

Bertha Muzzy Bower was the first writer to make a living writing popular westerns. Today's reader might think her an unlikely author of such a masculine genre; a Montana mother of three, she began writing short stories in 1900, desperate for money that would allow her to leave an unhappy marriage. That same marriage—to a cowboy employed by the McNamara and Marlow cattle company—gave her access to material for which eastern magazine editors were particularly keen: stories about ranch life and cowboys. After four years of typing stories in the tiny cabin she shared with her husband and three children, Bower's first novel, *Chip of the Flying U* (1904), became an instant hit, the first of over sixty novels and hundreds of short stories that would entertain millions of Americans for many decades to follow.

Bower's biography is worth reading not simply because of her role in founding a beloved American cultural tradition but also because of its inherent richness and drama. Indeed her life story resembles and anticipates later notable women writers of the American West, including Judy Blunt, Annie Proulx, and Joan Didion—to name a few—making her a foundational figure in a tradition of women's western writing that continues to thrive. Like Blunt, Bower wrote about ranch life in order to escape it, yet she also honored it in her fiction through exacting attention to realism and strenuous resistance to the sensationalism that quickly overcame the genre she helped to establish. Also like her successors, Bower's biography demonstrates the drama to be found in the everyday life of a western woman. Never staying in one place for more than a few years, Bower moved from place to place either in flight from personal or financial crises or in pursuit of opportunity. Embracing all things new and modern, Bower funded an aviation school for her favorite son, who had been captivated by the Wright brothers' first flight. When an old friend tracked her down with stories about a lost Mexican silver mine, Bower founded a mining company, hoping for a bonanza that never materialized. She built—or paid others to build—a retreat near Quincy, California, where she could both write and entertain her movie industry friends. Like Annie Proulx's Bird Cloud, the Pocket ranch failed to proceed as planned; guests overstayed their welcome, and Bower was left jaded and in debt.

Through all of these daily dramas, Bower wrote. She could always count on her writing to see her through periods of setbacks, finance a new business venture, or cover some unexpected expense. Not only her own survival but that of her extended family depended on it. Bower's writing saw them all through periods of family breakdown, medical and mental health crises, and job loss. Writing was also an endless labor. Bower spent most of her life on a writing treadmill, churning out novel after novel to keep herself afloat through both unwise expenditures and unforeseen economic turmoil, including the 1929 stock market crash that left millions of Americans destitute—Bower among them.

Among Bower's daily battles were frequent sparring matches with her risk-averse publishers. Fearing a reader backlash should her gender be publicized, they kept Bower's identity under wraps and urged her to churn out as many *Flying U* stories as they could print. Bower had other ideas: she wanted more public exposure and, when she became bored with westerns, took on subjects as various as bootlegging, mining, filmmaking, and deep-sea trolling. More often than not, her publishers discouraged these experiments.

In Bower's time, conditions weren't favorable for writing about her own experiences. She didn't have time for more than terse diary entries, and the market didn't value the felt daily life of a western woman, however remarkable her exploits and achievements. Both her daughter and granddaughter made attempts at biographies—in the 1960s and 2000s, respectively—but faced both personal and socioeconomic obstacles to their completion and publication. Since these attempts, however, certain orthodoxies about western writing have shifted. Judy Blunt, Joan Didion, and Annie Proulx have written powerfully about their experiences as women and writers in the American West. Reconstructing Bower's felt daily life as it is documented in her diaries, letters, and family papers, this biography claims B. M. Bower as their progenitor: a woman, writer, and western maverick whose daily life proved as dramatic as her fiction.

A Note on the Text

This book includes extensive quotations from personal letters, notes, and other unpublished documents. To preserve the feel of these documents as the stuff of everyday life, in most cases I have retained nonstandard usage and punctuation appearing in the originals unless changes were needed for readability. Typed and handwritten letters in the early twentieth century used underlining to convey emphasis. This has been changed to italics to translate that emphasis into print.

ACKNOWLEDGMENTS

I would like to thank Reed Doke and Bill Bower for trusting me with the story of their grandmother B. M. Bower and for sharing their family stories with me. Reed Doke was an attentive host as I spent several days poring over his grandmother's archive in his cheerful sunroom. Dele Newman Doke and Katherine Baird Anderson, daughter and grand-daughter of Bower, each wrote their own Bower biographies, both of which, though unfinished, proved enormously helpful in the writing of this book. The community of scholars at the Western Literature Association provided a jovial and helpful sounding board for testing early drafts of individual chapters. Christine Bold, Mary Chapman, Cathryn Halverson, and Jennifer Tuttle read drafts and offered encouraging and helpful feedback. Hope Houtwed's thoughtful and acute copyediting improved the manuscript immensely. I am also deeply grateful to the University of Nebraska Press for their ongoing support of my work. My partner, John Straube, has helped this project in innumerable ways, from caring for our pack of border collies (five as I write this, plus a miniature dachshund) while I am away for conferences and research trips, to tolerating my obsessive-compulsive habits when I am working and my television addiction when I am not. My colleagues and students at the University of Waterloo have provided a nurturing and stimulating community in which to carry out this work. The Charles Redd Center for Western Studies provided funding to support my research travel, and the staff at the Houghton Library at Harvard University helped me navigate their extensive publishers' archives. I have also been helped by librarians and archivists at the Glenbow Museum,

Margaret Herrick Library, and the Montana Historical Society. While I feel very fortunate to be in a profession where I get paid to teach, learn, and write, I am also grateful for my close friends outside of the academy, Viki Kidd and Marie Sawford, both avid readers and lifelong learners who, like me, have a lot of dogs. Their curiosity about Bower's life helped me write a story that I hope will be enjoyed by everyday readers as well as scholars.

THE BOWER ATMOSPHERE

1

An Unbearable Servitude

Bertha Muzzy Bower was living in close quarters in a tiny cabin in a hayfield near Big Sandy, Montana, when she made her first serious foray as a professional writer. It was the winter of 1900, and Bertha shared the drafty, three-room cabin with her husband and three children. Her husband, Clayton, had been hired to feed calves for the winter for the McNamara and Marlow cattle company, among the largest cattle operations in Montana. In exchange for forking hay to five hundred calves twice a day during the harsh Montana winter, Clayton received a wage and use of the small cabin on the TL ranch, part of McNamara and Marlow's extensive holdings in the state. Deeply resentful of her dependency on Clayton, and having from a young age nursed ambitions to become a writer, Bertha saved enough money to buy a typewriter, paper, and other supplies she would need to embark on a career as a professional writer. On December 15, 1900, she made the trek to town to post her first submission, a short story called "The Backsliding of Sister Stewart," to *McClure's Magazine*.

It was an opportune time for budding writers, especially from the West, because of a perfect storm of technological and social transformations that had been unfolding since the end of the Civil War. Print technologies made it possible to mass-produce magazines using cheap "pulp" paper, which could be widely distributed thanks to the expansion of the national railroad system. These same railroads brought millions of Americans to the big cities in search of factory work— another product of the technological boom. As American life became more urban and mechanized, readers craved stories about adventure and open space. So magazine editors, scrambling for quality content to fill their publications, looked West. Taking advantage of these conditions, a Montana housewife named Bertha Muzzy Bower became B. M. Bower, one of America's earliest and most important authors of that most macho of genres: the western.

In keeping with the mythology she would have a hand in creating, Bower would credit her success as a writer to her pioneering ancestors: "[My parents] gave me Sioux outbreaks for bedtime stories, and some real pioneer blood in my veins, and for these I am grateful."[1] Her father, Isaac Washington Muzzy, encouraged Bower to read widely. A Civil War veteran and direct descendant of *Mayflower* colonist Miles Standish, Washington and his wife, Eunice (Miner) Muzzy, homesteaded on railroad land in Le Sueur County in the new state of Minnesota in 1858. The Muzzys' settlement was in the thick of the traditional territory of the Wahpekute and Wahpeton, two subgroups of the Dakota, who were actively defending their homeland from encroachment by settlers like the Muzzys.[2] Bower's older siblings entertained her with tales of close encounters with the Dakota, none of which lived up to common stereotypes of Indigenous violence. On one occasion a Dakota man suffering from the severe cold arrived at their door and was given a pair of Washington's socks to wear.[3] Dakota resistance was met with brutal force in 1862 with the massacre, by the U.S. Army, of thirty-eight Dakota men in nearby Mankato. Eunice's father, who lived nearby, attended their public execution by hanging.[4]

Washington and Eunice had ten children, of whom Bertha, born in 1871, was ninth. Washington was an autodidact and polymath who, at various points in his life, worked as an architect, carpenter, farmer, soldier, and legislator. We know considerably less about Eunice—the lives of women settlers were rarely as well documented—but she was also a descendant of early colonists, as well as revolutionary soldiers, and she likely influenced her children in profound ways that we will never know. "She had need of this enduring inheritance," her granddaughter Dele wrote, "during her life with my grandfather."[5] It was

Eunice who supported the family while Washington fought for the Union in the Civil War. Of the many tasks that fell to her, weaving was the one her children would remember best. She was constantly at her loom, weaving colorful fabric to make blankets and clothing for the large family. As Eunice wove, the Muzzy girls picked burrs out of raw wool, spun it into yarn, and knitted stockings, scarves, and mittens.[6]

The American pioneer myth celebrates hardworking families who gradually transform wilderness into prosperous farms, but in reality, settlement was a speculative prospect depending as much on luck as hard work. Many settler-colonists were unable to make their farms pay because of conditions beyond their control. The post–Civil War era saw periods of economic turmoil fueled by rampant speculation on the rapidly expanding railroads, exacerbated by adverse environmental conditions, such as drought and pests. The Muzzys were among many midwestern families hoping for a share of the railroad bounty once the promised railroads were built, only to lose their farms after the bank collapse known as the Panic of 1873. In 1875 they left their farm in Le Sueur County and moved to Mower County, where they would live for six years, relocating to Otter Tail County in 1881. Adding further stress to these uncertain economic times, Washington Muzzy—whose health was compromised as a result of his Civil War service—was often unable to work and struggled to support his large family, sometimes having to take menial jobs as a farm laborer.[7] Despite their precarious finances, the Muzzys valued self-improvement, especially through literacy and reading, and were active in their community. Washington and Eunice helped found the First Baptist Church in Otter Tail County, and Washington joined the Farmer's Alliance and was elected to the state legislature in 1885.

Young Bertha Muzzy showed early signs of her independent nature and facility with language. As a toddler left to her own devices Bertha once took it upon herself to take a batch of goslings to the pond to join the other geese for a swim. By the time she was discovered by her older sister Vine, "she was on her second trip with two more goslings, dead, hanging from her chubby hands."[8] At the age of eight she gave a public recitation of the poem "Chickens" by Rose Terry Cooke. Vine remembered the event:

> She stood there on the school room platform, with her red-gold hair in finger curls around her head. She had on a dark dress, with a sash tied in a big bow at her back, and the sun shining thru the big window on her like a spot-light. She was as calm and self-possessed, as tho she was eighteen instead of *eight years old*. She "spoke her piece," with never a break and that big audience fairly raised the roof, when she had finished speaking the poem called "Chip and Peep."[9]

Of her nine siblings, Bower was particularly close to her younger brother, Newton, nicknamed Chip for his love of potato chips. The two youngest Muzzy children were close in age and still at school together by the time their oldest siblings had left home. When Bertha was eleven, the two sat together for a studio portrait in which the older Bertha stands with a protective arm around Newton. Later Bertha would name the hero of her first novel after him.

As busy as Washington Muzzy was supporting a large family while remaining socially and politically active, he found time to impress upon Bertha the importance of books, knowledge, egalitarianism, and public engagement: "My father taught me music and how to draw plans of houses (he was an architect among other things) and to read 'Paradise Lost' and Dante and H. Rider Haggard and the Bible and the Constitution—and my taste has been extremely catholic ever since then."[10] Bertha's first attempts as a writer showed the influence of living in an intellectual household: "I think the first of my efforts that actually appeared in print was a philosophical discourse on some heavy subject when I had reached the wisdom of thirteen years. It was published in a monthly farm magazine in which also appeared later some more contributions from my pen, together with a woodcut supposed to be my portrait. The picture was so atrocious, I remember, that it caused me to weep copiously and put a damper on my literary ambitions for the time being."[11]

The young Bertha also showed early signs of the sociability that would set her apart in adulthood. By the time she was eleven she had a calling card with her name in a flourishing script bordered by flowers and leaves in pastel colors. Bower's social aspirations must have been tempered somewhat by the realities of living in a large settler family where the drudgery of daily chores was a fact of life. This theme emerges in one of her earliest stories, "The Strike of the Dishpan Brigade," in which two sisters go on strike to protest the burden of washing breakfast dishes for a family of nine.[12]

When Bertha was seventeen, the Muzzys were enticed once more by the promises of a newly minted state: Montana. Most of Bertha's siblings had married and therefore remained in Minnesota. Only Bertha, her sister Kate, and her brother Chip made the trek to Montana on the recently completed rail route. Washington—well past middle age by now—and Kate filed on adjacent sections of land (a common strategy for expanding the size of the family settlement) a few miles from Great Falls, in the thick of Montana cattle country. There, Bertha, who had taught school shortly before the family left Minnesota, found work as a teacher. Her daughter Dele would later recall Bower's stories from her teaching days: "Some of her pupils were rough boys older and taller than she was. She tried to look fierce and maintain a discipline that would conceal her trepidation. She had a very dignified way about her, and a stern look that quelled rebellion. She told me once, with a twinkle, 'They may have been too big for me to spank with a switch, but thank goodness *they* never found that out! I just looked them in the eye and they toed the mark!'"[13]

Among the Muzzy's new neighbors were Lewis and Harriett Bower and their four sons. Clayton, the second youngest, caught Bertha's eye.[14] Among Bower's descendants, there are slightly different versions of what happened next. In one version, Bertha saw the handsome Clayton as an opportunity to seek escape from the drudgery of settler life and her parent's authority.[15] In another, Bertha ran off with Clayton to spite her sister Kate, who also had her eye on the young man.[16] Both versions agree that Bertha and Clayton eloped. Their marriage license is dated December 19, 1890.[17] Ten months later, their daughter, Bertha Grace, was born, followed by their son Harry in 1893 and Roy in 1896.[18]

Bertha and Clayton were ill-suited for each other. Clayton was happy to live from one payday to the next on a cowboy's wages, supplemented by any seasonal work he could come by. The gregarious and ambitious Bertha chafed at domestic life. She liked socializing, and her popularity with other men made Clayton jealous.[19] Nonetheless they managed to stay together for fifteen years.

However unhappy, Bower's marriage to Clayton proved fortuitous in one respect: it introduced her to the Montana cowboy community, which would become crucial to her later success as a writer. In a literary climate influenced by the rise of the daily newspaper journalist, magazine editors looked for fiction writers with firsthand knowledge of their subject, and Bower came to know cowboys from a unique perspective that resonated with readers. She differed from Owen Wister, whose novel *The Virginian* is widely considered the foundational western, and Zane Grey, who would be her chief rival author of serial westerns, by learning about cowboys from living among them as a social equal rather than observing them from a tourist's distance. Wister was the guest of wealthy Wyoming cattleman Frank Wolcott, and Grey traveled west on numerous fishing and hunting trips. The cowboys Wister knew were employees of his host and would have been expected to treat him with formality and deference.[20] Zane Grey modeled his cowboys after film characters, having never met any in real life.[21] In contrast to both of these men, Bower spent fourteen years living among Montana cowboys, most of them working for McNamara and Marlow.

Cowboys have fascinated people around the world since the brief period of the post–Civil War cattle frontier, when large cattle herds roamed freely on the open ranges of the Great Plains, creating employment for young men who were needed principally to manage the spring and fall roundups, when new calves would be branded and castrated, and mature steers were gathered for shipment to the East. Spurred by images of cowboys in dime novels, Wild West shows, and on cigarette cards, a popular mythology developed around this figure of virility and independence—a uniquely American version of the medieval knight-errant. Because cowboys remain a staple of television and film, we know—or think we know—a lot about them, but the mythology tends to downplay the more mundane realities of their work and culture.

According to Jacqueline Moore the term "cowboy" originally referred to the laborers who worked for large corporations and were considered the social inferiors of the "cattlemen" who owned the cattle and controlled most of the land they grazed.[22] Nevertheless cowboys' skills at riding, roping, branding, and castrating gave them some leverage over their employers, many of whom were absentees with little practical knowledge of cattle or ranching.[23] They shared a distinct culture vividly described by Moore, marked by activities like public consumption of alcohol (with every cowboy responsible for the purchase of at least one round), reckless spending, gambling, and risk-taking.[24] Their exposure to women was limited to sex and dance hall workers on the one hand and "respectable" women on the other.[25] The latter were usually the wives and daughters of cattlemen, whom cowboys treated with formality and courtesy.

Although cowboys are associated with open range cattle ranching, this mode of cattle management was short-lived. By the time Bertha eloped with Clayton, ranchers were already realizing that open range ranching was unsustainable. Cattle could not survive a bad winter, grazing lands needed management, and calves did better when they were kept close to home and fed regularly.[26] With these changes, the cowboy lifestyle lost some of its glamour. Cowboys were still needed for spring and fall roundups on the ranges that remained, branding and castrating calves and sorting out steers to be shipped. They were also needed for the decidedly less heroic work of forking hay to feedlot steers. These duties did not require the nomadic lifestyle so closely identified with the cowboy. Because cowboy labor was seasonal, many cowboys worked other jobs to make ends meet.[27] Clayton Bower, for example, worked as a deliveryman.[28] Bud Cowan, an acquaintance of the Bowers who we will hear more about later in this book, worked as a hotel clerk.[29]

Clayton Bower was somewhat of an anomaly in the cowboy community, where marriage was relatively uncommon. It was frowned upon by cattle companies and beyond the means of most cowboys' salaries.[30] As a married woman, Bower commanded more respect than the "disreputable" women most cowboys were used to, but as the wife of a cowboy, she had more opportunity to interact with cowboys than other "respectable" women. Bower may not have joined in on roundups, hunting trips, or saloon adventures, but she bore witness to the everyday lives of cowboys that sensational depictions overlooked, including evenings of music and dances that were the primary forms of recreation in rural western communities. During the winter the Bowers held musical evenings at their home: "A bunch of cowboys wintering in camp . . . used to come about once a week to the house to sing and play. I sang very well, my husband . . . played a guitar and sang. There was a fellow who fiddled, another who played banjo, and Bud [Cowan] who played guitar, mandolin, and piano if [available]."[31] The Bowers also attended dances, where Bertha's company was sought after, married or not. Bower's popularity at these gatherings would become one of the bones of contention when her relationship with Clayton began to crumble.[32]

Bertha was especially observant of the various forms of humor that were integral to cowboy culture and functioned both as entertainment and social ritual. Cowboys not only played pranks on and teased each other as an expression of social equality and belonging but also pranked and teased outsiders as a form of initiation or to challenge social hierarchies. Inexperienced cowboys or "tenderfeet" were subject to pranks that weeded out any unfit for the job. They might be told tall tales about the dangers of the job or be given the most unruly horses to ride. "Dudes"—upper-class easterners sojourning in the West—were subject to pranks intended to outwit them. One "dude" was sold the tip of a crowbar and was told it was a Comanche arrowhead.[33] Bower wove all of these complex and nuanced forms of humor into the fabric of her cowboy novels, creating what her publisher would call "the Bower atmosphere."[34]

While Bertha's ability to capture the daily lives of cowboys would eventually make her famous, there were sides to Bower's Montana experience that would prove less easily adaptable to popular storytelling. Her marriage to Clayton was not a happy one. Both Clayton and Bertha were pressured by social codes and economic realities in ways that generated conflict between them. Clayton's work as a cowboy was seasonal and precarious, making it difficult for him to live up to his masculine role as a provider, and he struggled with alcohol—a problem that preoccupied western activists in a region where saloons were an integral part of cowboy culture.[35] As a mother of young children with little access to paid work of her own, Bertha lacked even the minimal agency that Clayton had as breadwinner. Long after their deaths, when their marriage and breakup became the stuff of family lore, their descendants would describe their relationship using familiar narratives of family breakdown: some blamed Clayton, describing him as a poor provider and an abuser; others would hold Bertha responsible as an overly ambitious and critical wife of a husband who was doing his best in difficult circumstances.[36] The undoubtedly more complex reality is inaccessible to us, but Bertha did go on to represent the perspective of a woman in an unhappy marriage in her 1912 novel *Lonesome Land*.

Lonesome Land is a remarkable novel particularly because it challenges the conventional belief that early twentieth-century popular magazines only published formulaic pap and avoided difficult social issues. Written once Bower had several successful novels under her belt, *Lonesome Land* took on the topics of alcoholism and domestic abuse. The heroine of *Lonesome Land*, Val Peyson, is enticed by her beau, Manley Fleetwood, to leave her comfortable eastern home for a life with him on his western cattle ranch. In his letters Manley promises her an idyllic, pastoral home nestled in fertile western lands, but Val arrives at "a barren little habitation inclosed in a meager fence of the barbed wire."[37] At first Val tries to make the best of it but gradually loses her tolerance for Manley's drunkenness, neglect, and verbal abuse. Bower depicts the decline of their marriage through powerful scenes of growing domestic tension. The following passage takes place midway through the novel, when Val and Manley's relationship has disintegrated irreparably. The scene begins familiarly enough, with the vision of a cowboy at sunset: "With a blood-red sun at his back and a rosy tinge upon all the hills before him, Manley rode slowly down the western rim of Cold Spring Coulee, driving five rebellious calves that had escaped the branding iron in the spring. Though they were not easily driven in any given direction, he was singularly patient with them, and refrained from bellowing epithets and admonitions, as might have been expected." Bower contrasts Manley's patience with the cattle with his harsh treatment of Val: "'Open the corral gate!' he shouted to her, in the tone of command. 'And stand back where you can head 'em off if they start up the coulee!'" Silence is the only way Val can think of to manage her volatile husband: "She was not in the habit of wasting words upon Manley; they seemed to precipitate an unpleasant discussion of some sort, as if he took it for granted she disapproved of all he did or said, and was always upon the defensive."[38] To distract herself from her intolerable situation, Val focuses on a plan of escape: "She was not thinking of Manley at all, nor of his mood, nor of his brutal coarseness. She was thinking of the rebuilt typewriter, advertised as being exactly as good as a new one, and scandalously cheap, for which she had sold her watch to Arline Hawley to get money to buy. She was counting mentally the days since she had sent the money order, and was thinking it should come that week surely."[39] Val hopes the typewriter will be her first step toward becoming a writer and gaining independence from Manley: "It's intolerable having to ask a man for money," she explains. "There seems to be money in it, for those who succeed, and it's work that I can do [at home]."[40]

Bower's account of her own beginnings as a writer is similar, if in fewer words: "I was living in Montana, keeping house for my husband and my three little tots. . . . I had started writing in the hope that I could earn enough to support myself and my children so that I dared free myself from a despicable bondage."[41] At the time Bower describes, the Bower family was living in the hayfield cabin near Big Sandy. In this remote cabin, the musical evenings with the cowboys stopped.[42] The family of five was crammed into three small rooms an hour's walk from town, with no neighbors or other distractions to deflect the growing tension between Bertha and Clayton.

Bower's writing activity is one aspect of this period of her life that she documented meticulously. She adopted a businesslike approach that she maintained throughout her career, probably influenced by trade publications like *Authors Magazine*, which published fiction and poetry by new authors, offered advice to aspiring writers, and sold ads for typewriters, ink, paper, advertising schools, and the like. *Authors Magazine* was part of a national boom in products and publications capitalizing on the magazine revolution of the 1890s, which made writing careers more accessible to working-class people.[43] Bower also took a workmanlike approach in the way that she adopted a daily writing regimen that she would keep up for the rest of her career. We know about this regimen because Bower recorded almost every story she wrote, its word length, where it was submitted and published, the feedback it received, and how much it earned. Her manuscript record books were among the few documents to survive Bower's regular document purges, demonstrating the importance she would attach to her identity and history as a professional writer.

Bower began to write seriously during that winter at the cabin, while Clayton forked hay to McNamara and Marlow's calves and her two oldest children were probably in school. She wrote her first stories in longhand until she was able to buy a secondhand typewriter, much as Val does in *Lonesome Land*.[44] Bower's fingers must have ached from the cold as she wrote or typed in the drafty cabin. Virginia Woolf had not yet penned her famous essay "A Room of One's Own" (1929) when Bower planned stolen moments for writing while Clayton and the children were away or asleep. Or perhaps she was able to shut out the activity around her, quietly writing while the rest of the family occupied themselves as best they could in their cramped and isolated cabin. When he wasn't forking hay, Clayton might have read, chopped wood, hauled water, stoked the fire, or perhaps visited the saloon in Big Sandy. The older children, when they weren't in school, likely helped with the chores, played cards, or read whatever books, newspapers, or magazines might be on hand. One imagines the constant tap of Bower's typewriter in the background and wonders if it became a source of conflict when it took Bower's attention away from Clayton and the children.

On December 15, 1900, Bertha made the first of many journeys through the bitter Montana winter to the post office in Big Sandy and mailed her first story, "The Backsliding of Sister Stewart," to *McClure's*, one of the top nationally circulating periodicals of the day.[45] Without waiting for the reply, she quickly started work on a second story, "The Ghost in the Red Shirt." On January 6, 1901, "Backsliding" was returned with a "kind personal letter" that was positive enough to encourage Bower to revise the story. She completed "Ghost" and submitted it to *Rough Rider*, a small western magazine that was just beginning publication in Butte, Montana. That story was promptly returned to her with a rejection slip on March 1, but the undeterred Bower promptly sent it to another magazine the next day and kept working on her third story, which she submitted to *McClure's* on March 14. She continued to write new stories while receiving a steady stream of rejections. When the latter came with personal letters rather than slips, she doggedly accepted the feedback, revised the story, and sent it to the next publisher on her list. One story was submitted eleven times in three years before it was finally published. She kept this up for the next year, fitting her writing into her daily routine of chores, childcare, and tense exchanges with a husband she could barely stand.

After almost two years of persistent submissions, rejections, and revisions, Bower received her first acceptance. The 3,500-word story "When the Salt Has Lost Its Savor," her sixth, completed in July, was accepted in October 1902 by *Authors Magazine* for a payment of twelve dollars. It was on the low end of the pay scale for short fiction but a healthy sum nonetheless—about a week's wages for the average Montana schoolteacher.[46] With the roundup over and another winter setting in, Bower wrote a Christmas story that was immediately accepted by *Authors Magazine* and published that December. *Authors Magazine* accepted four more stories by May 1902, but Bower lost this tenuous foothold in the magazine fiction market when *Authors Magazine* suspended publication later that year. Still, during the first half of 1902, Bower was producing new stories and finding new venues for existing work in the western publications *The Coast* (Seattle) and *The Argonaut* (San Francisco).

Yet another year passed with little success. Indeed Bower stopped writing new stories altogether over the winter of 1902, resuming in the spring of 1903 with "The Maid and the Money," a romance between a class-conscious young woman and a cowboy. It was accepted by *Ainslee's* for a healthy sum of thirty-five dollars, along with a request for more stories.[47] This proved to be a turning point for Bower, not only because *Ainslee's* was a nationally circulating publication that featured reputable authors but also because *Ainslee's* publisher, Street & Smith, was in the midst of launching a new pulp magazine. *The Popular* was an experimental magazine featuring "quality" fiction in a cheap pulp format traditionally identified with fiction for juveniles.[48] Something about the cowboy story by an author living in the thick of cowboy country caught the *Ainslee's* editor's eye.

With her most significant publication to date and the promise of more to come, Bertha could finally take a break from her strict writing regime. In late August 1903, Bower treated herself and the children to a holiday in Tacoma, Washington, where Chip, married in 1897, had recently moved with his wife, Elvina, and their three children.[49] The Bowers and the Muzzys visited Bower's brother-in-law Owen Bower on Fox Island, where Owen was clearing land for a ranch. Family photos show the two families piled atop an enormous redwood stump, rowing in Puget Sound, and gathering windfall apples from the ground.[50] These informal and impromptu photos are a departure from the stiff studio portraits of earlier years, a visual sigh of relief after three years of hard writing start to bear fruit.

While Bower was grinding away at short stories that paid anywhere from one to twelve dollars, an upper-class Philadelphian trained as a lawyer published a cowboy novel that was topping bestseller lists. Owen Wister's *The Virginian* was published in May 1902 but had been based on short stories appearing in slick magazines during the 1890s.[51] While most cowboys were too busy doing the work of managing cattle to have time to write fiction about it, the well-connected Wister was paid to write fiction based on his western travels. With the help of an extensive ad campaign, *The Virginian* made bestseller lists and reached a national readership that included the McNamara and Marlow cowboys. One of them, Scottish Canadian Bertrand "Bill" Sinclair, was unimpressed.[52] He was annoyed to see an outsider appropriate the cowboy's story, and he wondered "why no cowpuncher ever wrote about his own time and his own people—instead of leaving it to outsiders, however observing, however sympathetic."[53]

Nicknamed the Fiddleback Kid—not because of any musical ability but because his horse bore the Fiddleback brand—Bertrand Sinclair arrived in Montana at the age of seventeen and soon gained a reputation for his abilities as a bronc rider:

> I ambled into Big Sandy astride a free-stepping roan and went to work for Tingleys. . . . Babe Tingley handed me out a chunky black. He tried to slip his pack, and failing that, stampeded through a four-strand barb wire fence and then jumped into an irrigating ditch and bogged himself down in the muck. And that was my ruin, because word got around that I could ride, and wherever I went during the seven years I worked on roundup, they handed me mean ones, and I didn't have sense enough not to try and get in the middle of them.[54]

Despite having little access to formal education, Sinclair was interested in a wide range of topics, including sociology and philosophy.[55] He liked poker and whiskey as much as the next cowboy, but he also used his spare time to work on assignments for correspondence courses.[56]

During the winter of 1902 or 1903, Sinclair was hired by McNamara and Marlow to help Clayton feed their winter steers.[57] He boarded with the Bowers, bringing their numbers to three adults and three children that shared three small rooms.[58] Despite the nine-year age gap between them, the thirty-year-old Bertha had much in common with the younger boarder. They were both aspiring authors and avid readers, self-taught in many subjects, and fond of conversation. The two began a partnership that would boost both authors' careers. After Sinclair returned from forking hay, Bertha would show him her work, and his feedback helped her accurately depict the details of cow-punching.[59] Bower returned the favor by sending Sinclair's first story to a publisher. It was accepted, and Sinclair used the money to buy new spurs.[60] Bertha would later assert that their beginnings as writers were integral: "I can't tell of one without telling of the other, too, for both are intermingled."[61]

Descendants and other observers have speculated about whether or not Bertha and Bertrand's relationship became sexual while he stayed at the cabin. Bower insisted that her relationship with Sinclair "was as fine and clean a relationship as a man and woman can have."[62] However, at least one family story maintains that Bertha's affair with Bill triggered Clayton's rage and the eventual disintegration of their marriage.[63]

With encouragement from both Sinclair and *Ainslee's* editor Charles MacLean, Bower spent the winter of 1903–4 perfecting stories of ranch life in Montana. After her first publication in *Ainslee's*, the magazine rejected Bower's next six submissions, but these rejections were accompanied by personal letters to Bower that helped her revise her work. Bower finally managed to give MacLean what he was looking for with "At the Grey Wolf's Den," submitted in December 1903 and accepted in February 1904 for fifty dollars. It was Bower's first story of the fictional "Flying U" ranch, of which many more would follow. The story appealed to popular fascination with the American West without pandering to the sensationalism of Wild West shows and dime novels—a characteristic that would set Bower apart throughout her career. "At the Grey Wolf's Den" satisfies dominant expectations of western fiction to dramatize the conquest of the wilderness by American "civilization," but Bower does so in relatively mundane terms, describing in detail how westerners tracked and killed wolves and coyotes as a backdrop for a courtship plot featuring a cowboy and a plucky western woman. A photograph exists of Sinclair having done something similar, a stunned coyote at the end of his rope while he looks on from astride his horse.[64] In both cases, the scene takes place in winter, when bored cowboys turned predator control into a sadistic form of amusement. Such detailed accounts of western life fascinated eastern readers, many of whom lived in crowded cities and worked in secretarial or factory jobs, but they also appealed to rural and western readers who appreciated the authenticity of detail in Bower's fiction. A Montana reviewer would praise her ability to paint vivid scenes of ranch life "without resorting to the many hackneyed characters and situations which characterize so many of the latter-day tales of the West."[65] Wyoming journalist Ted Olsen wrote, "She does know her west. Her cowboys are something more than clothing dummies draped in chaps and wicked rowels."[66]

Emboldened by the sale of another Flying U story, titled "Why Weary Went A-wooing," for which Bower received another big check (for seventy-five dollars), she began work on a novel, *Chip of the Flying U*. While Clayton and Bertrand fed the TL calves, Bower typed. During breaks, Bertha and Bertrand discussed her project while Clayton, excluded from their writers' banter, must have been fuming. Bertrand "read 'Chip' hot out of my little typewriter," Bower later recalled. "We talked about the story whenever he came into the house."[67] Local landscapes, ranches, and characters become fodder for Bower's fictional Flying U ranch. According to Sinclair she modeled it after the local TL, whose brand was a flying *A*, called so because the *A* was drawn with horizontal tips or "wings" on either end, and whose cowboys were the prototypes for some of her characters.[68] However, years later, when Bower received inquiries about the location of the "real" Flying U, she would insist that both the ranch and its cowboys were fictions with only a loose basis in the settings and people she knew. "I'm terribly sorry . . . but please believe the author, who should know, *there is no original Flying U ranch* such as I described in all my stories. I wish there were. . . . A fiction writer draws upon life and trained creative imagination for all characters. Or should." Bower did eventually disclose some of the locations that inspired her. She based the fictional town of Dry Lake on Big Sandy. "The hotel . . . , store, 'Rusty Brown's saloon,' the blacksmith shop, and the road out of town through the lane, I described as well as I could. The country is real, the characters, no!"[69]

However firmly Bower insisted that the Flying U stories were works of her imagination, she prided herself on the authenticity of her fictional cowboys. A much-contested concept, western authenticity was and is variously defined, but for Bower it meant the accurate representation of cowboy life and work and close attention to atmospheric detail. From the very beginning, *Chip of the Flying U* makes plain Bower's disdain for the violent West that proliferated in dime novels and newspapers— the West that was mythologized in *The Virginian*'s defense of vigilante violence. Bower counters these conventions by opening *Chip* with a lynching—a fake one, staged to pass time on the cowboys' Sunday off and terrify a "tenderfoot" female visitor scheduled to arrive later that day. As the cowboys plan their prank, popular cowboy stereotypes become the stuff of satire:

"We'll dig up all the guns we can find, and catch up the orneriest cayuses in our strings, and have a real, old lynching bee—sabe?"

"Who yuh goin' t' hang?" asked Slim, apprehensively. "Yuh needn't think I'll stand for it."

"Aw, don't get nervous. There ain't power enough on the ranch t' pull yuh clear of the ground. We ain't going to build no derrick," said Jack, witheringly. "We'll have a dummy rigged up in the bunk house. When Chip and the doctor heave in sight on top of the grade, we'll break loose down here with our bronks and our guns, and smoke up the ranch in style. We'll drag out Mr. Strawman, and lynch him to the big gate before they get along. We'll be 'riddling him with bullets' when they arrive—and by that time she'll be so rattled she won't know whether it's a man or a mule we've got strung up."[70]

Female stereotypes are equally lambasted. The cowboys expect the visiting Della Whitmore—who has just completed medical school—to either "faint away at sight of a six-shooter, . . . buy her some spurs and try to rope and cut out and help brand," or "round us up every Sunday and read tracts at our heads." The real Della does none of these things. After proving herself an excellent shot by shooting a coyote on her way to the ranch, she and her escort, Chip Bennett, spy the "lynching" unfolding in the distance:

A chorus of shouts and shots arose from below. A scurrying group of horsemen burst over the hill behind the house, dashed half down the slope, and surrounded the bunk house with blood-curdling yells. Chip held the creams to a walk and furtively watched his companion. Miss Whitmore's eyes were very wide open; plainly, she was astonished beyond measure at the uproar. Whether she was also frightened, Chip could not determine.

The menacing yells increased in volume till the very hills seemed to cower in fear. Miss Whitmore gasped when a limp form was dragged from the cabin and lifted to the back of a snorting pony.

"They've got a rope around that man's neck," she breathed, in a horrified half whisper. "Are—they—going to HANG him?"

"It kinda looks that way, from here," said Chip, inwardly ashamed. All at once it struck him as mean and cowardly to frighten a lady who had traveled far among strangers and who had that tired droop to her mouth. It wasn't a fair game; it was cheating. Only for his promise to the boys, he would have told her the truth then and there.

Miss Whitmore was not a stupid young woman; his very indifference told her all that she needed to know. She tore her eyes from the confused jumble of gesticulating men and restive steeds to look sharply at Chip. He met her eyes squarely for an instant, and the horror oozed from her and left only amused chagrin that they should try to trick her so.

"Hurry up," she commanded, "so I can be in at the death. Remember, I'm a doctor. They're tying him to his horse—he looks half dead with fright."

Inwardly she added: "He overacts the part dreadfully."[71]

No Bower character invited more speculation about his origins than Chip Bennett, the cowboy hero. He bore little resemblance to his namesake, Bower's brother Chip, who was not a cowboy. According to one rumor, Bower modeled her hero after western painter Charles Russell, illustrator of the hardcover version of *Chip of the Flying U*, but the two had not yet met when *Chip* was written.[72] Bud Cowan would also claim to be the real Chip, much to Bower's annoyance. After years of questions, Bower would finally admit to a resemblance between Chip and Bertrand Sinclair: "I did not, as a matter of fact, consciously use any one cowboy for any of my Flying U characters. After *Chip of the Flying U* was written, however, I could see that Chip was very much like Bill Sinclair."[73] Like Sinclair, Chip is seriously injured while trying to break a horse and is left unable to ride. While Sinclair used his time off from the roundup to travel in order to audit English courses at the University of Washington, the bedridden Chip fills his time by completing a painting begun by Della.[74]

The central plot of *Chip* is also reminiscent of the relationship between Bower and Sinclair as developing writers. Whereas Sinclair served as Bower's first reader, Chip helps Della complete a painting of a western landscape. The collaboration, however, is not an equal one: Bower makes clear that Chip is responsible for the authenticity of the scene.[75] In this sense *Chip* might be said to subscribe to the notion that men are best equipped to write of the "real" West. However, as an upper-class, privileged woman from the East, Della is far from Bower's fictional double. Her privileged eastern origins are the more salient liability here. Moreover, Bower manages to carve a space in her novel for the West she was most familiar with as a wife and mother; the subject of Chip's painting is a winter scene of a starving cow defending her calf from a pack of wolves. If Bower could not break through as a writer by explicitly depicting the perspective of a mother in the West, this illustration at least hints that cowboys were not the only ones in the West with a story worth telling.

The cowboys of Flying U ranch, which Bower dubbed the Happy Family, serve as the backdrop for a budding romance between Chip and Della. Moral prohibitions prevented Bower from depicting the bawdier aspects of cowboy culture, but she loved to poke fun at their masculine facade. Despite—or perhaps because of—the shortage of women in the West, cowboy communities sometimes replicated heteronormative social structures, complete with certain "feminine" roles. Photographs survive of cowboys dancing with each other when female partners were in short supply. Certain occupations, such as that of the cook, were also feminized.[76] This play with gender would feature prominently in Bower's novels. Each of the Happy Family cowboys has a distinct set of characteristics and foibles, often signaled through ironic nicknames. Happy is a pessimist, Slim is short and fat, and so on. While Owen Wister took the masculine code very seriously, Bower represents cowboy masculinity somewhat satirically; her cowboys, even the most heroic ones, are fallible and vulnerable and keep secret anything about themselves that might compromise their masculine image. Chip Bennett hides the fact that he is a talented artist for fear his brethren will ridicule him for his effete pastime. Andy Green is the best rider at the Flying U, but unbeknown to the other cowboys, he acquired his horsemanship skills as a circus rider clad in spangled tights.[77]

As Bower's career as a professional writer began in earnest, her marriage to Clayton continued to deteriorate. Between January and April 1904, Bertha received seven acceptances, including one for *Chip of the Flying U*. Initially submitted to *Ainslee's* in early April, *Chip* was diverted to *The Popular* as a circulation builder for the new magazine, now under the editorial leadership of Charles MacLean. She received $225, which must have felt like a massive sum. Her May 1904 submission, a short novel, was also accepted, for $150. "Success came all at once," she later reflected. "I'd been writing for several years with only fair success, then all of a sudden it seemed like every mail brought a check. Soon everything that I had written was sold, and editors were calling for more. It almost bewildered me."[78]

According to some accounts of Bertha's split with Clayton, her success exacerbated the tension between them. Clayton felt entitled to more than Bertha was willing to share, even bragging that she was his "little red-headed gold mine."[79] Clayton was already abusive to Bertha and the kids, and he got worse as Bertha asserted her independence and control over the money she earned.[80] Other Bower descendants believe that Clayton was not abusive by nature but felt neglected by Bertha, who had always liked male company, and may have been "stepping out" on Clayton.[81] It's likely that Clayton assaulted Bertha at least once—an incident that Bill Sinclair would later relate to his nephew.[82] Perhaps this scene in Bower's 1912 novel *Lonesome Land* was based on her own experience of domestic violence:

He had her by the throat, shaking her as a puppy shakes a purloined shoe. "I could—kill you for that!"

"Manley! Ah-h-h—" It was not pleasant—that gurgling cry, as she struggled to get free.

He had the look of a maniac as he pressed his fingers into her throat and glared down into her purpling face.

With a sudden impulse he cast her limp form violently from him. She struck against a chair, fell from that to the floor, and lay a huddled heap, her crisp, ruffled skirt just giving a glimpse of tiny, half-worn slippers, her yellow hair fallen loose and hiding her face.[83]

As soon as Bower secured her first writing contract, she made her move. *Chip of the Flying U* ran as the lead story in the October 1904 issue of *The Popular*. Editor Charles MacLean hoped it would build circulation of the fledgling magazine, and it did so "with a bang."[84] Bower was offered a contract for six stories at seventy-five dollars each, which she signed in January 1905. Subsequent events remain a subject of discussion and debate among Bower's descendants. Bower's granddaughter Kate Baird Anderson would do her best to figure out what happened, piecing together documents with fragments of oral history gleaned from interviews with locals about the time "Bert Bower ran away with Fiddleback."[85] She believed that Bower made plans to leave Clayton as soon as her contract with *The Popular* gave her the financial security to do so. She arranged for the children to spend another holiday in Tacoma, waited for Clayton to leave for the spring roundup, then boarded a train for Great Falls, Montana, where her mother and sister lived after Washington Muzzy died in 1896.[86] There, she divorced Clayton and, on August 12, 1905, married Bertrand Sinclair in a small ceremony at her mother's home.[87]

Bower eventually sent for little Roy to join her in Great Falls, but her two oldest children, thirteen-year-old Bertha Grace and eleven-year-old Harry, went to live with Clayton's parents, who now lived in Spanaway, Washington.[88] Clayton was reunited with his children shortly after Bertha left—presumably in Washington—and the three remained close.[89] By 1910 all three lived in the same neighborhood in Chehalis County, where Harry worked in the local cannery, and Bertha Grace had recently married the cannery manager Martin Wingarter.[90] Soon after her marriage, she emigrated to Australia, never to contact Bower again.

Some of Bower's descendants regard Bower's choice to leave Harry and Bertha Grace behind as a callous act of abandonment, while others maintained that she did the best she could under difficult circumstances.[91] It may be that Harry and Bertha Grace chose to stay with their father rather than join their mother and her new husband. In any event, to dwell too much on Bower's parenting applies a double standard that male authors generally do not face. Owen Wister never faced the difficult choice between children and career because his wife, Mary Channing Wister, bore the brunt of the responsibility for childcare among a long list of other tasks.[92] Zane Grey was an incorrigible womanizer throughout his marriage, yet this has not undermined his legacy as an author.[93] Nevertheless it must have been traumatic for Harry and Bertha Grace to lose their mother, only to be constantly reminded of her whenever her name appeared in bold letters on the covers of popular magazines.

2

A Brief and Stormy Passage

After their marriage, Bertha and Bill moved into a small house in Great Falls, where Roy would join them. Located by its founder near the falls of the Missouri River, the ideal location for a hydroelectric plant, Great Falls was carefully laid out in a grid system, with parks and tree-lined streets. By the time the Sinclairs lived there in 1904, the power plant had served its purpose, fueling rapid industrial growth that included a silver and copper smelter.[1] The town's main amenities included a store, post office, bank, newspaper, saloon, rooming house, various services, and a selection of shops selling furniture, clothing, and other goods.[2] While the town offered considerably more diversions than the Bowers' hayfield cabin, Bertha would not be distracted. Having completed her first contract with *The Popular*, she was working on a new one writing for *Ainslee's*, signed shortly before her marriage in August 1905. These were exclusive contracts that forbade Bower from writing for other magazines, but between contracts she still squeezed in submissions to other venues.[3] Meanwhile the Bower name was becoming firmly entrenched in Street & Smith publications. Throughout 1906, a Bower story was published every month in either *Ainslee's* or *The Popular*. Her pace was furious; she could finish a six-thousand-word story in two or three days. Bill's career was also developing but at nowhere near the pace. Having given up cowboying to focus on writing, he was more selective than Bower about the venues he wrote for, aspiring to break into the more prestigious slick magazines. Like Bower, he wrote outdoorsy adventure stories set in exotic and rugged locations.[4]

Much of Bower's output consisted of Flying U stories in which she developed the cast of characters at the fictional Flying U ranch. These included Weary, a "tall, good-looking cowboy"; Pink, "boyish looking, but dynamite in action"; and Cal Emmett, with "big blue eyes, likes the girls, argumentative, boastful."[5] The demand for these stories in *The Popular* seemed insatiable, but Bower also had literary aspirations. She particularly admired Wharton and Dickens, referencing their work in her short story "The Hall of Mirth" and her novel *Lonesome Land* through the unhappy couple that lives in Bleak Cabin. Knowing full well that *The Popular* was not the most prestigious venue she could aim for, Bower squeezed in submissions to the "slick" magazines—so called because they were printed on expensive "slick" paper—in between contracts for Street & Smith. These efforts were not as successful, but she did manage to publish a story called "The Long, Long Lane" in the *Smart Set*, a magazine "for and about New York's social elite" that published the likes of Jack London and Theodore Dreiser.[6] "The Long, Long Lane" embraced the magazine's critical stance toward popular trends by depicting the dissonance that Bower and many westerners experienced between western myth and their own lived experience. Her protagonist is an impoverished cowboy barely able to keep up payments on his failing homestead. As he regards a standard western landscape scene, he feels a sense of entrapment rather than freedom: "On the ridge a gray wolf howled plaintively the hunting call. Across on the farther hillside a coyote yapped back impertinently. Straight ahead, the little, round corral lay empty, and beside it, in the low, sod-roofed stable, he could hear a horse sneeze the hay dust from his nostrils. And in his heart he hated it all with a hatred that rose up in futile rage against the circumstances that held him there."[7]

While the *Smart Set* provided Bower with an outlet for her more highbrow aspirations, as a woman who had only recently raised herself out of poverty, Bower could not ignore the money to be made from *The Popular*. As she would later reflect, "My market absorbed everything as fast as I could turn it out, and I fear I followed the line of least resistance."[8] Nonetheless Bower was able to take another step out of the pulp world when *Chip of the Flying U* appeared in book form in

April 1906. Like magazines, books had also become more affordable in the early twentieth century, and home libraries were becoming a sign of respectability for the growing ranks of the American middle classes. Intended not just for reading but to enhance the appearance of a library, shelf, or side table, many books featured colorful dust jackets and well-wrought illustrations. *Chip* was illustrated by one of the best: cowboy artist Charles Russell, a friend of Bill's from his cowboy days whose studio was in Great Falls—not far from the Sinclairs. The Sinclairs socialized often with Charles Russell and his wife, Nancy, paying visits on horseback to Russell's log cabin studio and admiring the western scenes that covered the walls from floor to ceiling.[9] Like Bower and Sinclair, Russell was making a good living from serving the popular fascination with the American West. Born in St. Louis in 1864, Russell moved west in 1880, and he worked as a cowboy while establishing himself as a western illustrator. In this sense, he, like Bower and Sinclair, depicted the West from a working cowboy's vantage point. By 1897 he was earning enough from his artwork to set up a studio in Great Falls.[10] His paintings deeply impressed Bower as the most authentic of any western artist of the day. She would later tell her publisher, "For me there is only one Western artist, and that is Russell. He knows the life and locality of which I write, you see . . . [the West has] been part of his life for many years."[11] So determined was Bower to have Russell illustrate the book edition of *Chip of the Flying U* that she agreed to pay half of his fee. One of Russell's three illustrations for the novel was his interpretation of Chip Bennett's painting—called *The Last Stand*—of the cow protecting her calf from a pack of hungry wolves. Russell had painted a similar scene, called *Waiting for a Chinook*—now on display at the Gilcrease Museum in Tulsa, Oklahoma—inspired by the devastation of the winter of 1886–87, when entire herds of cattle died. The painting became "the talk of Montana Territory" because of how powerfully it captured the worst winter in recent memory.[12] Surely this was the painting Bower had in mind when she described *The Last Stand* in *Chip of the Flying U*.

The hardcover edition of *Chip of the Flying U* was an immediate and long-lived success. Positive notices and heavy publicity by New

York publisher G. W. Dillingham Company resulted in strong sales, and it would remain in print throughout Bower's lifetime. Anxious to keep hold of their new star author, Street & Smith signed her to a third contract—this time for three years, although Bower made sure to negotiate the right to submit to other publications.[13] Despite the fact that her pen name now appeared in bookstores and newsstands all over the country, few people aside from friends and relatives knew that Bertha Sinclair was a successful author. A local newspaper report on the publication of *Chip* in hardcover revealed only that the novel was written by "a Great Falls woman under the pen name of B. M. Bower."[14]

Bower's low profile was likely at the behest of her editor at *The Popular*, Charles MacLean. Whereas she published earlier stories—including "The Maid and the Money" and "Guileful Peppagee Jim"—as Bertha Muzzy Bower, this would change when she began writing exclusively for Street & Smith, where she was known only as B. M. Bower and was assumed to be a man by most of her readers.[15] As Bower would later explain, "The idea that B. M. Bower is a man has been carefully fostered ever since my Western stories began to attract attention. Mr. MacLean of the POPULAR is very much averse to having my identity revealed."[16] Particularly because *The Popular* was still new and in the process of defining itself, Charles MacLean did not want to alienate the audience that was still believed to constitute the bulk of pulp readers: adolescent boys.

By keeping her full identity under wraps, however, MacLean was compromising Bower's stature as an author. Pseudonyms were for "hacks" who published in quantity for money; "real" authors made their identities known to the public. In all likelihood MacLean over-emphasized the extent to which Bower's gender threatened her success. Other women such as Caroline Lockhart, Vingie Roe, and Catherine Newlin Burt would write western novels in their own names. Indeed the macho, violent western that we know today did not exist in 1906 outside of the dime and nickel novels written for boys.[17] Furthermore the pulp fiction market was changing. Accessible public education had expanded after the Civil War, increasing literacy rates and fostering a more sophisticated readership for cheap fiction.[18] The so-called respectable magazines were too expensive, and the cheap dime novels were too juvenile and sensational. A new niche for fiction was emerging: adult readers of low-priced but "quality" fiction. These readers were not so invested in the masculinity of their western authors, but the young MacLean was averse to taking risks with his newly discovered property. The tug of war between MacLean, who did not want to tamper with a successful brand, and Bower, who wanted publicity, recognition for her accomplishments, and the freedom to experiment, would continue for much of Bower's career.

Bower pushed back against MacLean's regime of secrecy in December 1906 by granting an in-depth interview to the *Great Falls Tribune*. "Two Great Falls Authors of National Fame," the bold headline shouted from the top of the page. Beneath it, large portraits of Bower and Sinclair eradicated whatever was left of Bower's anonymity—in Great Falls, at least. "The names of B. M. Bower and Bertrand Sinclair are known to thousands of people outside of Great Falls," the article began, "where they are known to one person in this city, and this despite the fact that the people bearing these names have been residents here for several years."[19] The article went on to disclose not only Bower's real name but also her address, removing all doubt of the identity of B. M. Bower. The interview further revealed that Bower's pen name was a subject of negotiation with her publishers, but she downplayed her gender as the main issue. Bower explained that when she married Sinclair, she had wanted to change her pen name to B. M. Sinclair, but because she "was well known as a writer under [B. M. Bower], her publishers were unwilling to let her change it, unless gradually." The article continued: "So she now uses the name, B. M. Bower, with B. M. Sinclair in parentheses under it. 'I hope to be allowed to discard the other name entirely in time,' said Mrs. Sinclair, smiling." However, this would not be the case. Bower's publishers soon dropped any reference to the Sinclair name, and B. M. Bower she remained.

As the first and last in-depth piece about Bower ever published in her lifetime, the *Great Falls Tribune* article provides us with a rare glimpse of the Sinclairs' daily life as Bower rose to fame, painting a portrait of a writer struggling to keep up with demand while editors' requests poured in. Some compared her to other star authors of the day: "The editor of a well known magazine in New York had watched her work with interest [and] could think of no other short story writer that he had known, who had developed literary power as rapidly as had she, with the one exception of O. Henry." Quotations from fan mail included in the *Great Falls Tribune* article provide us with the only surviving documentation of early Bower readers, including evidence that women, as well as men, enjoyed her western stories:

> Dear Sir: I am interested in your stories by B. M. Bower, and is he living? Is his stories true? Is there such a place as Dry Lake, Montana? Is there any boys by the name of Weary, Chip, Cal, Jack Bates, Happy Jack, Shorty, Slim and J.G. Whitmore? Do they live at the Flying U ranch?
>
> The reason why I am asking these questions is that a lot of us young girls are going to Montana later on to be Wild Westers ourselves, and probly we'll visit them if there are any such people.

In addition to supplying a window into Bower's experience with her first real taste of success, the *Great Falls Tribune* article affords us a glimpse of her plans for the future: "They both prefer the country to city life, and it is their intention to remove in the spring to their ranch in the eastern part of Valley country, where they will continue their literary labors and raise horses as an avocation." The Sinclairs' planned ranch would enable them to continue to live the lifestyle they wrote about, which both authors considered integral to their craft.

The *Great Falls Tribune* article did not disclose the fact that, in December 1906, Bower was heavily pregnant and due to deliver in late January. Indeed her belly had grown so big she could barely reach the typewriter. Still, she kept writing, completing stories on December 14 and January 2. On January 25, 1907, she gave birth to a daughter, Della Frances Sinclair, named after the plucky heroine of Bower's first novel. Della was born during a fierce blizzard that gripped northern Montana. Heavy snow blocked rail routes and caused significant losses of livestock.[20] Indeed, the winter of 1906–7 would be remembered as the worst cold spell in twenty years.[21] This may explain why Bertha and Bill did not follow through on their plan to settle on a ranch and write stories. They may have been among the many ranchers who lost their livestock that winter. It would be Bower's last winter in the harsh northern Montana climate. By the fall of 1907, Bill, Bertha, Roy, and baby Della had moved to Santa Cruz, California.

Both Bill and Bertha had ties to California. Between roundups, Bill had audited courses at Stanford and taken advantage of its library.[22] Bertha's uncle Marcus Alonzo Miner lived in the San Joaquin Valley along with his large family. California boosters touted the state as "the land of sunshine," full of boundless opportunity, a healthy climate, and a diverse and exotic culture. In addition to all of these advantages, the Sinclairs could continue to cultivate their identities as western writers with access to lots of natural space for horseback riding, fishing, and hunting—all without Montana's harsh climate.

In Santa Cruz, the Sinclairs rented a two-story house overlooking the ocean, with a large shaded porch, generous yard, and plenty of room for Della and Roy to play with their pet dog. They decorated their living area with photographs of their Montana cowboy days and Charles Russell paintings, and they lined their mantle with books. Della—who went by Dele in adulthood—would later recall feeling "surrounded with everything that spells harmony, with parents who sang and told original stories, gave in to every slightest whim, and spoiled me rotten."[23] For writing, Bill and Bertha set up a "den": "a large sunny room on the second floor at the top of a narrow stairway," Dele remembered. "It contained all the necessary writing equipment by twos—two typewriters, two easy chairs, two lamps—hundreds of books, a Victrola, for music was as essential as food to these two creative individuals." The writing den was "forbidden territory" to the children. "No one must intrude upon their morning regime of writing."[24] Bill took an occasional break from the typewriter to roll a cigarette or check on Dele and Roy in the yard. Bower settled into a routine of writing two novels a year plus short stories almost monthly for *The Popular*, with the novels issued in hardcover by Dillingham. Her contract kept her too busy to shop stories around with more prestigious periodicals—a circumstance that she would later regret—but it enabled the Sinclairs to live very comfortably. They could afford hired help for cooking, cleaning, and childcare, as well as modern luxuries like the Victrola, which they played all day long. While Bertha wrote steadily under her contract with *The Popular*, Bill pursued more prestigious "literary" venues while writing less and making less money. In public they presented themselves more conventionally, the 1910 census suggests. They concealed their nine-year age difference, reporting Bertha as thirty-six to Bill's thirty-three, and they identified Bill as an author and "head" of the household, while Bertha was given no occupation.[25] Her identity as B. M. Bower was still largely under wraps, although one newspaper did identify "Bertrand Sinclair and wife" as "two noted story writers."[26]

In addition to domestic comfort, Santa Cruz offered the Sinclairs a widening social circle and access to diversions such as the theater, shopping, and an intellectual community. After a morning of writing, Bower would spend the afternoons with family and friends.[27] One family photo shows Bower and little Dele in their horse-drawn carriage, stylishly dressed for social calls. Bill enrolled in courses at Stanford and attended debates at local salons. He became particularly good friends with author Stewart Edward White, son of a wealthy family who had since become an author of outdoor adventure stories and a practitioner of "the strenuous life"—a lifestyle involving extensive exercise and outdoor activity. White introduced the Sinclairs to local authors and actors whom the Sinclairs enjoyed entertaining in their Santa Cruz home.[28] Among the Sinclairs' theater friends was actor and theater manager Leo Chrystal, who had gained notoriety in California papers when he disappeared in the midst of a dispute over his inheritance: a ranch worth $100,000—a fortune at the time. During his absence, Chrystal had traveled to Hawaii and Australia, "doing trapeze stunts in a circus for a living, taking orders in an antipodean coffee-house, [and] hiking over the bush with sheep-shearers."[29]

It was on a visit to the ranch located in the Carmel River valley in California that Chrystal stood to inherit that the Sinclairs got the idea for their first writing "camp" in the spring of 1909. For all of the opportunities afforded them in Santa Cruz, their comfortable situation presented a challenge to the Sinclairs as writers who emphasized adventure and authenticity of place. Bower in particular had built her reputation on her strong attachment to Montana—an attachment she did not have with California, with its very different climate, terrain, history, and culture. This would be a paradox throughout Bower's career: how to continue to write from a position of local knowledge and authority when her circumstances removed her from the settings and communities she was most closely identified with as a writer. Her editors in particular tended to pressure her to stick to cowboys long after Bower's interest was drawn to other topics.

During their visit to his (future) ranch, Leo Chrystal brought the Sinclairs to a nearby abandoned dairy farm, located in a deep canyon accessible only by a steep, narrow, and winding road.[30] Neighbor Emilie Girard later described the site in terms that convey its storytelling potential:

> All that remained were two dilapidated cabins, a barn and pig sheds. . . . A short distance from the cabins there was . . . a spring of water, bubbling out of the rocks, looked some what like a grotto, there were prickly pears around the rocks too. . . . The Pedrazzi family [who had settled the area] had gathered rocks big and small from the area and built rock fences around the cabins. . . . They also had a small grape vineyard on a side hill, and a few fruit trees.[31]

The "forlorn setting brought forth immediate story ideas," so in June of 1909, Bertha, Bill, Roy, and Dele set out for the place Bower nicknamed "Hungry Hollow."[32] Although Dele was only three years old at the time, she would later write vividly of that summer camp—no doubt drawing heavily on family photographs and lore. She made the trek there on the front of Bower's saddle astride Bower's beloved riding horse Babe; eleven-year-old Roy rode a fractious riding mule called Angel Face, and the family's supplies and provisions, including two typewriters, were carried on their pack mules Wise One—so named because he had once eaten pages out of an encyclopedia—and Doodad.[33] It was to be a working holiday—especially for Bower, who was still writing under a demanding contract with Street & Smith.

At Hungry Hollow, Bower continued to write in the mornings while the others rode, hiked, swam, hunted, and fished. While she continued to set her fiction in Montana, she used Hungry Hollow as a thieves' hideaway in her short story "The Dry Ridge Gang" and based some new Happy Family characters on people she met in the area.[34] Bill was not so productive in terms of authorship. "I think her husband was not too full of the desire to write stories during this long pleasant summer," Dele reflected. "He was not under contract to meet a publisher's deadline, so he was found oftener than not along the clear streams ribboning the country nearby, casting his favorite flies into the deep pools where luscious mountain trout lay deep in the shadows. Then there was deer hunting, and trophies to prove his skill." Still, the fish and game that Bill and Roy brought home fed the camp, enabling Bower to focus on her writing.

Dele's account of the summer at Hungry Hollow suggests the spot served its purpose well as a space where Bower could perform the life of which she wrote—unlike the upstairs office in her comfortable Santa Cruz home. Many hours were spent on "leisurely rides down unknown trails leading to tucked-away cabins," wrote Dele. "My mother was always appropriately dressed in her western version of what the fashionable horsewoman wore. The Stetson was really a Stetson, with the horsehair hat band and belt, and the quirt my father made."[35] Photos from that summer show Bower engaged in traditionally western activities. One depicts her at target practice. "She was an expert with any kind of fire-arm," Dele's annotation reads, "a sharpshooter who knocked tin cans off posts with ease of perfect coordination." Another shows Bower about to mount the stolid and sturdy Babe, clad in appropriate western riding garb: a split riding skirt—"she never wore slacks ever," Dele writes—silver spurs, and a braided leather belt. Dele's annotation describes her as "an expert judge of horseflesh." Little Dele was also initiated into the western lifestyle, photographed under a grape arbor wearing Bill's Stetson hat and six-gun holster, holding a rifle longer than she was tall.[36]

After a winter in San Jose, California, where the Sinclairs had rented a sprawling, turreted Victorian home, the family returned to Carmel in 1910 for another summer in camp. This time they camped on the banks of the river on a property belonging to the Girard family, whom they had befriended the previous summer. Joining the Sinclairs at camp was Bower's son Harry, whom she had not seen since she left Clayton Bower in 1904.[37] Harry had been working in a cannery in Westport, Washington, where Clayton—now remarried with a baby daughter—also lived.[38] Called the "bloomer" camp because it had been used by a party of women in bloomers, it was less remote than Hungry Hollow and had amenities for campers.[39] The easier access enabled the Sinclairs to bring more of the creature comforts they had become accustomed to in town, so they loaded their pack mules with tents, carpets, typewriters, furniture, books, staples such as flour and salt, and Bower's beloved Victrola. In a clearing shaded by mature trees, they set up separate tents for sleeping, eating, and writing, all facing a central common area comprised of a firepit surrounded by a few mismatched chairs. A hammock on the edge of the camp provided space for napping, reading, or quiet reflection. When her Victrola wasn't playing in her writing tent, Bower set it on a chair in the center of camp, where it could supply background music for chores, card games, or conversation around the fire.[40]

The Sinclairs' relatively accessible location allowed for more companionship than at the more remote Hungry Hollow camp. Photos from the summer suggest the Girards were frequent companions on picnics or visits to the Girard farm. Dele and Roy, sometimes joined by the Girard children, participated in classic activities for early twentieth-century kids in the country: rafting on the Carmel, playing with the Girards' kitten, and helping care for a fawn orphaned when Bill accidentally shot its mother. Dele cried for days after having to leave the fawn behind when the Sinclairs returned to town.[41] Hiking excursions enabled the Sinclairs to further relive the strenuous life they celebrated in their fiction. One particularly difficult trek became a little too strenuous when the party, according to a note written by Bower herself, "ran out of grub" and "lived three days on venison with salt" until "Daughter

Dear [Dele] kicked the salt can into the river." Then the horse got away and they "walked back, fording 'by hand' the Carmel, *29 times*."[42]

Like the previous writing camp, Bower kept to a consistent schedule of writing while Bill spent more time fishing and hunting with Harry and Roy. Bower's luxurious writing tent was designed for someone who spent many hours in it. It had a wooden floor lined with Navajo rugs and a stove for heat in the cool mornings. Its furnishings consisted of a desk, a writing stool, and a reclining wicker chair. This setup enabled Bower to take breaks from her spartan typing stool to recline in the wicker chair while she went over her manuscripts or wrote rough drafts in longhand. Next to her desk she placed a stand for her Victrola, which pointed in her direction as she worked. A photograph widely circulated on the internet depicts her perched erect at her desk, eyes trained on a clipboard that must have contained the handwritten draft she was transcribing. Bower's annotation on the photograph tells us that this was where she wrote *Lonesome Land*, her most autobiographical—and daring—novel yet.[43]

Bower made her reputation by providing an original alternative to the sensational West depicted in dime novels, but her earlier work still catered to her editor's conception of the popular taste for "interesting" plots with a "strong love interest" and a positive resolution. Although Bower insisted that firsthand knowledge enabled her to craft realistic characters, settings, and subplots, much of her experience—including her unhappy first marriage—was not fodder for popular storytelling. *Chip of the Flying U*, for example, featured a romance between a feisty heroine and a laconic cowboy that culminated in their avowal of love. *Lonesome Land* was a groundbreaking departure from such norms for popular representation of marriage, written at a time when Bower was established enough to write more experimentally.

In place of the idealized romances characteristic of her earlier work, *Lonesome Land* contains many parallels to Bertha's own unhappy marriage to Clayton Bower. The novel also addresses other aspects of western life commonly overlooked in popular magazines. Its male antagonist is drunk when we first meet him, and over the course of the novel, he descends into what today's readers would recognize as alcoholism.

The female protagonist Val Peyson fears she will lose her sanity from the loneliness of life in a remote cabin, and, in the novel's climax, is violently attacked by her estranged husband. And although there is a male protagonist—a cowboy named Kent who offers Val companionship and support during her difficult marriage—he does not rescue her in the end. While Val decides to divorce her husband, she also refuses Kent's lovemaking.

Whether Bower was aware, as she wrote *Lonesome Land*, that her own marriage was unraveling around her is a matter for speculation. According to Bill's biographer, Betty Keller, Bill and Bertha were not well-suited from the start, despite all that they had in common as western writers. Bower's independence did not accommodate her domestic life, and Bill had married Bower without realizing what he was getting into. With time it became clear that each wanted different things from the marriage. Bower wanted a writing partner and companion and was less interested in the physical side of marriage than Bill was. Bill was not as prolific a writer as Bower, and he "resented his wife treating him as if he were her protégé."[44]

The exact circumstances leading to Bertha's split with Bill remained a family mystery that took two generations to unravel. After recording the submission of *Lonesome Land* in the fall of 1910, Bower stopped making entries in her manuscript record book and would not resume for another two years. Just four years old at the time of the divorce, Dele would not learn the details of her parents' separation until just before Bower's death, when Bower "let slip a few comments here and there that put together gave quite a picture." Dele refused to reveal what she learned when she wrote her own biography of Bower in the late 1960s: "I would NOT I REPEAT NOT descend to the sensationalism most biographies are or were promoting. . . . So the ms was written in a stilted, skimming-over-the-surface-of-intimate-situations-slant."[45] Thus she wrote cryptically, "The Bower-Sinclair trail began to waver and fade into the shadows. . . . It was evident that the trail was going to reach an impasse. . . . I know now the reasons for all this, but it died with them. So be it."[46]

Nor did Dele share whatever knowledge she had with her children. Her daughter, Kate Baird Anderson, spent years trying to get to the bottom of the breakup when she made the second attempt by a Bower descendant to write Bower's biography. In 1993 she wrote in her notes that Bertha and Bill began "to pull in separate directions, two naturally sensitive, reticent people, stubborn and strong-minded."[47] As her research continued, however, the mystery was partially solved. In 1999 she wrote to a librarian that "a violent disturbance . . . appeared in the form of a pretty young relative of [Bertha's]."[48] A year later Kate wrote a more fleshed-out version of the story: "The Bower-Sinclair partnership ended the summer of 1911 when [Bertha's] pretty young cousin, a gorgeous but self-centered girl, visited camp, threw herself at handsome Bill and got pregnant."[49] The cousin in question was Ruth Miner, eighteen years old at the time, daughter of Bower's uncle Marcus Alonzo Miner.

Sinclair's biographer offers a slightly different version of the story. It was not at camp that the affair began, according to Betty Keller, but after the Sinclairs returned to St. Jose, when Ruth and Lydia, another Miner cousin, came to visit. Keller's version better aligns with available evidence. Photographs show the party of four on a trip to Yosemite in the Sinclairs' new Buick, beginning Bower's lifelong love affair with the automobile. One photograph shows Lydia and Ruth posing with Bill by a picturesque waterfall. Other photos, likely taken by a fellow tourist, show the party of four arranged in a tableau at the base of a giant sequoia, and in the Buick, parked in the hollowed-out belly of another of the giant trees.

In mid-September 1911 Ruth told Bill that she was pregnant. During what Bill described as "a brief and stormy passage," Bower grappled with the dissolution of what she had thought was an ideal partnership between two like-minded authors.[50] According to Keller, Ruth and Bower were the ones to decide Bill's fate: Bower would divorce him, and he would marry Ruth and take responsibility for the child he had fathered with her.[51]

3

A Lodge in the Wilderness

"It's Idaho for you, all right. I've taken lots of time and thought the thing over from all sides before deciding, and it seems the best we can do." So Bower wrote to fourteen-year-old Roy from Bliss, Idaho, in November 1911. The tiny town situated on the Snake River was Bower's refuge while she figured out her next steps after leaving Bill. A branch of the Miner family—including Bower's uncle Marcus Miner, father of Lydia and Ruth, and her aunt Lydia Miner Bliss (married to David Bliss, founder of the town)—had settled in the Snake River area after the Civil War. Bower and Dele would be staying at the ranch of another cousin, Frank Bliss.

Bower's letter to Roy hints at a hasty departure from St. Jose and much uncertainty about the future of Bower and her children. She gives Roy detailed instructions for the safekeeping of her books, Charles Russell paintings, and Roy's collection of hunting trophies, lamenting that their beloved horse Babe would have to stay in St. Jose. She asks him to bring gifts for their hosts: walnuts, oranges, and candy for Christmas gifts. "It's about all I will give," writes the cash-strapped Bower. During her time in Bliss, Bower planned to save enough for a fresh start in California the following year. Bower advised Roy to not waste money on a Pullman train car when second class was comfortable enough, and she instructed him to be sure to pack a lunch to save on "diner-grafters."[1] Throughout the letter, Bower simultaneously fusses over and reassures Roy, spelling out in granular detail the steps he must take on his two-day train journey to Bliss and glossing over the turmoil Roy must be experiencing at the prospect of losing his stepfather and friends, changing schools, and living with virtual strangers. "It will seem like home, here, after you get used to it, and you will like your relations, I am sure . . . I guess you can learn as much here as in San Jose, this winter, and have the pleasure of living in the country." She promises him opportunities for hunting ducks and quail with his younger relatives, and she dangles the prospect of a new horse if he can save enough on travel expenses: "Take for your mottoe, 'REMEMBER THE SADDLE HORSE' and save up for it."[2]

Bliss was a small town for which boosters held high hopes now that recent irrigation projects and a new bridge over the Snake River increased the potential for future prosperity and growth. It was equipped with the usual necessities, including two general stores, a hotel, a blacksmith, a livery, and a bank, and luxuries such as a restaurant and opera house. There were schools, an electricity provider, and three churches.[3] But it was a far cry from California. Although Bower claimed to like her new surroundings "better than [she] did at first" and that she "hate[s] to leave, now," her letter suggests she missed the perks of California life more than she cared to admit. Oranges in Bliss were "little, runty things . . . too expensive for a California lady to buy." The shopping also left much to be desired: "You've no idea what a cheap-john town this is, when it comes to having anything decent at decent prices."

The winter was a productive one for Bower even as she continued to recover from the devastation of the previous fall. She was given a "snaky cayuse" named Snip to ride and a board-and-batten shed to write in.[4] There, she completed another Montana novel, *The Uphill Climb*, about a cowboy who struggles with alcohol and ends up marrying a stranger during a drunken binge. Through situational humor, Bower had again found a way to make a less-than-idyllic West palatable for popular narrative. Then she turned to writing more short stories for *The Popular* and getting to know her new book publisher, Little, Brown and Company.

Bower's contract with Little, Brown represented a step up in prestige from the pulps and from G. W. Dillingham, her previous book publisher. Boston-based Little, Brown had been in business since 1837, publishing many classic works, including texts by Benjamin Franklin and George Washington. In discussions with Little, Brown about potential future book publications, Bower wrote rather apologetically about the quality of some of her work in *The Popular*: "I have written many stories that have never been brought out in book form; some of them are scarcely worthwhile—because I have done a great deal of work hurriedly, under pressure of the constant demand for magazine stuff from me."[5]

Bower's rising stature brought with it the opportunity for greater publicity and recognition, but MacLean's warnings about disclosing her identity still held sway. In preparation for publicizing their edition of *Lonesome Land*, Little, Brown asked Bower for biographical material, a request she demurred, stating, "Mr. MacLean, of *The Popular* is very much averse to having my identity revealed." The book publisher, however, did not see Bower's gender as the liability it was for *The Popular*. After all, *Lonesome Land* was a female-centered story, and the genteel Boston publisher was not so invested in catering to adolescent male readers as *The Popular*. Bower, however, passed up this opportunity to escape the closet MacLean had created for her. "You may say that 'Bower' is essentially a Western product. . . . 'Lonesome Land' is therefore familiar ground, and the people types that I know intimately. I have myself lived in 'shacks' upon occasion, and played my little part in the drama of the range. . . . All this does not bear the earmarks of femininity, does it?"[6]

Having been away from Montana for several years, using it as a setting became more and more tenuous given the importance Bower attached to her intimate knowledge of the places she wrote about. Her new book would be set in the Snake River Valley. Although the first draft was written for *The Popular* before Bower moved there, she revised it substantially for the Little, Brown edition while she was in Bliss, using her cousin's ranch as the basis for her fictional one.[7] With a title that references a hateful and racist slur, the novel engages with the history of colonial occupation in the area.[8]

The Snake River Valley was part of the traditional territory of the Shoshone-Bannock Tribes and the site of several decades of violent struggle, especially after the Civil War, when American fur traders and gold prospectors—including Bower's uncle Marcus Alonzo Miner, a gold prospector—flooded the area. Several decades of tribal resistance culminated in the Bannock War of 1878, after which the Shoshone-Bannock Tribes were confined to the Fort Hall Reservation. They nevertheless managed to become prosperous farmers and stockmen active in the local economy, so it was not unrealistic for Bower to depict the protagonist of her novel as a rancher of Indigenous ancestry.[9] Whereas the Shoshone-Bannock Tribes maintained many aspects of their traditional culture, however, Bower's protagonist has been entirely assimilated into settler society—a familiar trope in ostensibly sympathetic but actually racist representations of Indigenous people by white settlers of the period.

Bower and her publisher were particularly preoccupied with preserving racial categories underlying Indigenous speech, even though they disagreed about what that meant. Little, Brown felt that her new novel contained "too much Indian dialect spoken by the white people."[10] If the Boston publisher found it inappropriate for white characters to speak in a racialized dialect, then Bower believed communication between the two groups was impossible *unless* white speakers used dialect because of the inferiority of Indigenous speech and intellect: "As well make the negro in fiction speak good English, as the Western Indian—or the whites when speaking to Indians, for that matter."[11]

Although Bower presumed authority to represent the Shoshone-Bannock people as she saw fit, she was quick to object to distorted images of cowboys by outsiders. This becomes clear in Bower's negotiations with the motion picture company Selig Polyscope, which wrote to her just as she prepared to return to California in June 1912. Attracted to California by its mild climate, varied landscapes, and distance from Thomas Edison's eastern monopoly, Selig Polyscope had set up its Edendale, Los Angeles, studio in 1909 and was looking for material for its moving pictures. The studio offered Bower one hundred dollars for novel rights and seventy-five dollars for short stories. Bower replied with a list of stories she thought would be suitable, emphasizing "good action and setting," humor, and romance. While she did not object to the standard narrative devices required of popular stories, she nevertheless regarded herself as a guardian of western authenticity where cowboys were concerned: "I am going to beg you most earnestly," she implored the filmmaker, "to preserve the *atmosphere* of these stories in the event of your using them; by that, I mean not to overdress the cowboys—and especially not to let them drape their neckerchiefs over their bosoms; I never saw a puncher wear his like that, unless he was terribly drunk or wanted to look stagey."[12]

By July 1912 Bower had saved enough money to return to San Jose, California. Her career was thriving; *Lonesome Land* sales were brisk enough to warrant multiple printings, and Little, Brown was eager to publish future novels. Selig Polyscope had purchased the moving picture rights to several of her stories, including *Chip of the Flying U*, and she continued to write steadily for *The Popular*. She rewarded herself with a visit to her brother Chip in Tacoma that fall before returning to work on her next novel. Two portraits taken during this period offer clues about Bower's state of mind as she recovered from the personal setbacks of the previous year and reestablished herself as an independent, professional woman and single parent.[13] One of them, probably taken in late summer or fall of 1912, suggests the central role Roy had taken on not only as Bower's child but her companion. Bower is seated in a rustic chair made of rough-hewn tree branches, smartly attired in a Victorian, high-collared dress, hat, and gloves. Roy stands behind her, leaning casually into Bower's chair, wearing a suit, tie, and Stetson. They both look straight into the camera, unsmiling—in accordance with the style of the time. Although Roy was just fifteen when this photo was taken, the composition positions Roy as Bower's protector rather than her dependent.

The second portrait suggests Bower's growing confidence as an author who had graduated from anonymous pulp hack to respectable book author; a bare-shouldered Bower gazes past the camera from beneath a wide-brimmed, floppy hat. Beneath the image, her signature appears: "Sincerely, Bertha M. Sinclair, 1912." It is probably this portrait that Bower refers to in a letter to Little, Brown written in October 1912:

Since the identity of "B. M. Bower" is becoming more and more an open secret, I have decided to come out boldly and declare myself a woman writer who has succeeded in doing a man's work as a man would do it. It's bound to come soon, in spite of me, so that it is perhaps merely making a virtue of necessity.

. . . It has occurred to me as not a bad idea to use a cut of the author as the frontispiece of the next book. What do you think of it? If it appeals to you, I shall be glad to send you a late photograph which really is a good likeness. And if there is any other sort of announcement you would like to make . . . , I shall not hedge, as I did last winter.[14]

In contrast to Bower's formal portrait with Roy, the headshot she had in mind for book publicity suggests a different image of Bower as an author: independent, free-spirited, and unashamedly feminine. After a successful year professionally, Bower had the confidence to push back against MacLean's code of silence around her gender. Although Little, Brown "was not able to use" Bower's photo in her book, the publisher was keen to reveal her identity in their publicity and asked for "several different photographs" and "a biographical story" for that purpose.[15]

After *The Uphill Climb* was republished in book form, Bower ran out of old material to fulfill her contract with Little, Brown for two novels per year. In the fall of 1912 she began a new novel, *The Gringos*. For the first time Bower wrote a full-length novel set in California, her home for the last five years. The transition from Montana to the new setting did not come easily to her. Rather than represent the West as she experienced it, she set *The Gringos* in the immediate aftermath of the Mexican-American War, using familiar plot devices for representation of American settlement in former Mexican territory through two American settlers who fall in love with the beautiful daughter of a Spanish aristocrat. Bower enlisted the help of an early California settler, according to the novel's dedication to George W. Lee, "who furnished [her] with data, material, and color."[16] When it was finally finished in April 1913, she wrote, "Thank God the thing's done!" in her manuscript record book. Little, Brown was enthusiastic about the book:

"We are pleased to say that we consider it the strongest novel you have offered us."[17] Bower, however, felt that it was "out of [her] field" and therefore did not sound at all like a "B.M. Bower story."[18] Reviews for *The Gringos* were nonetheless positive and reflected the influence of publicity material disclosing Bower's identity: "In 'the Gringoes' [*sic*] B. M. Bower has written again of the West and of ranch life such as she knows so intimately and loves so well," wrote a reviewer for the *Oakland Tribune*.[19] The *Boston Globe* published a publicity photo of Bower alongside its review, praising the masculinity of Bower's writing: "The name [B. M. Bower] has stood over many stories of the West that have the firm grasp and the terse, clean-cut style usually attributed to a man."[20]

As was now her habit after finishing a big project, Bower celebrated the completion of *The Gringos* with time off for travel. In the summer and early fall of 1913, her travels took her to Seattle, possibly to visit Chip, and to Quincy, California, where she had an encounter that inspired yet another abrupt change of address. As she explained to her publisher:

> I have always wanted to find just the right place for a home in the wilderness, and in The Pocket Ranch I believe I have found it. Sometimes I say that while Jack London was writing about The Valley of the Moon, B. M. Bower ran across the very spot quite by accident and recognized the place at the first glance. This valley was settled away back in "The Gringos" time; and this little nook among the hills has been known as "The Pocket" ever since then as nearly as I can discover. It is surrounded by pine forests reserved by the government. Two trout streams run through it, there are glimpses of the hills and the blue of broad valleys between.[21]

In October 1913 Bower and Dele rented rooms at the Plumas House Hotel in Quincy while Bower negotiated the purchase of 100 acres of the 140-acre property.[22] She and Dele would stay in the existing house on the property over the winter while Roy stayed with Bill before moving on to relatives in Idaho. Bower wrote her editor with details of her plans: "I am going to have the best time of my life, I believe, turning the Pocket into my ideal of a lodge in some vast wilderness."[23]

In the Pocket, Bower envisioned not only a new home but also a site of inspiration for her writing. As much as she loved her new home in California, she had struggled to adapt her writing practice to San Jose's manicured landscapes and cosmopolitan influences. In *The Gringos* she had turned to an early historical period to evade the problem of how to make the transition to a California writer, but historical fiction proved an uncomfortable genre for her. She envisioned the Pocket ranch as an authentically "western" space in which she could reconstruct the conditions for authentic western writing as she understood it:

> It will be simple as the hills around it when all is done; no graveled driveways or fountains or foreign shrubs—it will be the wild adapted to my needs [illegible]. There will be a roomy log house built from the trees on the place, and there will be horses to ride, guns to hunt with, trout rods aplenty; and furthermore, there will be that old-time hospitality which asks no questions, the hospitality which is the very essence of the old Western atmosphere.[24]

That first winter at the Pocket proved less idyllic than Bower anticipated. The two rivers that flowed through the ranch, however scenic, flooded the property three times over the winter, hampering Bower's progress on her new novel.[25] She was also learning about the seamier side of the publishing business. She had gotten herself into trouble with Little, Brown for violating the terms of her contract, which stipulated that no Bower book could be published by another house within six months of a Bower publication by Little, Brown. Bower had sold some old Flying U stories to her old publisher G. W. Dillingham upon assurances from them that they would honor her six months contract with Little, Brown by waiting until her new novel *The Gringos* was published in the fall of 1913. However, Dillingham began taking orders for their Bower book that same fall, using the title *The Flying U Ranch* to leverage the stories for which Bower was most well-known and undercutting orders for *The Gringos*. In an apologetic letter to Little, Brown,

Bower blamed Dillingham for misleading her and assured the former that she would have no more dealings with them: "I do not consider their methods honorable and I should not want to be identified with them further."[26]

Bower was growing more confident in her dealings with Little, Brown, whose editors she never met and Boston offices she never visited. Her business rhetoric draws upon the same subtle irony as her fiction, both of which undercut the power of the urban East to define and dominate the rural West. She takes responsibility for her "blunder" without appearing incompetent or naïve, laying out the many steps she had taken to ensure the timely publication of *The Gringos* and gently reminding Little, Brown that they had contributed to the mess by publishing *The Gringos* late despite Bower's best efforts to get it proofread in time. "I don't know what you are going to do to me," she added, "but under the circumstances I don't think you ought to have me hanged." She concludes by hinting that her growing stature as a writer is tempting her with other options: "I have turned down a cash offer for the volume of old short stories which you would not want to publish, and which, being old work of mine would not technically come within our contract at all. . . . And since generous cash offers look pretty good to a person who is building a ranch out of raw scenery, I want you to know that I feel decidedly heroic right now in spite of my plight."[27]

Bower's first novel written at the Pocket returned to the now familiar setting of the Idaho countryside. Bower completed *Ranch at the Wolverine* in ten weeks, submitting it to *The Popular* on March 7, 1913, in time for spring publication. The $2,500 she received from *Popular* helped finance the construction of the new house, which, with the help of a crew of relatives and hired hands, had already begun. The crew consisted of Roy, Marvin Benson—who had recently married Bower's cousin Lydia Miner—a handyman named Tom, and a hired carpenter. They set up a campsite where they would live during construction, which Bower named "Dove Camp." Bower furnished her sleeping tent with a full-sized bed and decorated it with one of her Russell paintings—the original artwork for *The Last Stand* from *Chip of the Flying U*—and a pastel portrait of Dele. Directed by Bower, the crew cleared away the dense underbrush and debris brought in by the annual spring floods. They prepared a site for the house on a hillside dotted with evergreen trees, and the house's double walls were filled with sawdust for insulation. To prepare the fence line around the property, Bower used two axes to cut her way through the dense brush, climbing over logs and boulders as she went, ignoring the rattlesnakes that crossed her path as she marked the trail for the fence. Work started at about 8:45 a.m. each morning and lasted until 11:30 a.m., when they would cool off with a swim in the creek, and then they would enjoy a leisurely lunch until 1:45 p.m., when they would "get up and go poking off to work again."[28]

The finished product was both rustic and opulent. The main floor, built over a raised cellar to guard against flooding, was fronted by an enormous enclosed porch that overlooked the surrounding countryside. From the second floor, viewers enjoyed the same view from the gabled bedroom windows. Inside, the centerpiece of the house was a welcoming great room, large enough to host the lavish parties Bower had planned. An enormous stone fireplace, flanked by large windows, dominated the room. From above each window gazed one of Roy's hunting trophies, while Bower's collection of Russell paintings adorned the simple plank walls.

In early summer, to celebrate the completion of her new house, Bower held a housewarming for her new neighbors, who were excited about the prospect of a famous writer in their midst: "There was a big social event here on Saturday night [June 13]," the local paper reported, "when the whole town adjourned en masse to the home of Mrs. Sinclair to assist in a housewarming there. . . . She has erected a beautiful bungalow . . . and is now engaged in writing another book. This is to be her home in the future, and it is expected that many events and many scenes in Plumas County will find renown through her books."[29] Despite Charles MacLean's misgivings about revealing her identity, Bower's neighbors in Quincy knew from the start that Mrs. Sinclair was the author of the famous B. M. Bower books, and local boosters considered her presence a boon.

The Pocket ranch would be home to not only Bower but also numerous relatives and friends who stayed for both short and extended visits. Roy had married in April to a young woman named Kitty that he had met in Idaho, and the couple was now a part of the household. Although their courtship had lasted less than a year, they were so anxious to marry that they lied about Roy's age—he would not be of legal age to marry for more than a year—telling the local paper that he was eighteen. Bower, who was loath to deny her favorite child anything he asked, consented to the issuance of the marriage license.[30]

As much as she idealized her secluded "lodge in the wilderness," Bower was unwilling to spend another cold, wet winter at the Pocket. After completing *The Flying U's Last Stand*, another Flying U novel, Bower sent seven-year-old Dele to boarding school in Los Gatos, California, not far from St. Jose, and, by late November, she had rented an apartment at the Burlington apartment complex in Glendale, close to the Selig Polyscope studio. Bower's moviemaking connections had already been forged after several Bower books were adapted to moving pictures, including *Chip of the Flying U*. Disappointed with how other scenario writers adapted her work, Bower eventually negotiated to write them herself so that they would "not be warped into melodrama."[31] According to family lore, Bower's film work brought her into contact with Tom Mix, a leading actor for Selig Polyscope and star of the first film adaptation of *Chip* (released in 1914), as well as other Selig Polyscope performers. In the thick of Hollywood Bohemia, Bower developed a fascination for the emerging film industry and an ambition to become more involved in filmmaking. "It's a great business," she wrote prophetically to Selig. "I believe it has a bigger future than most people realize."[32] Having launched her career by transforming her experience among cowboys into the stuff of popular culture, Bower made that transformation new grist for her story mill.

Bower's life was now a far cry from what it had been in Montana. After four children and two marriages, she was an independent, single woman with the means to indulge her love for parties, travel, and fast cars. She kept very little documentation of this period, but family oral history and a few tantalizing fragments—fleshed out by cultural histories about early Hollywood—can at least provide a sense of her Hollywood phase. Dele would later tell her own children stories about their famous grandmother who lived in Hollywood and socialized with celebrities while Dele spent most of her days at a boarding school where she was miserable.[33]

Bower arrived in the Los Angeles area just as the city had transitioned from its reputation as the idyllic "land of sunshine" to the fast-paced home of the American film industry. Dozens of film production studios had been established in Los Angeles by the fall of 1914—not only the familiar names like Universal and Famous Players but also those largely forgotten after decades of consolidation of the industry: Lasky, Sawyer, Lubin, Vitagraph, and others. Attracted by opportunities as performers, writers, directors, journalists, office workers, drivers, and a myriad of other occupations, young men and women flocked to this emerging urban frontier, where they cultivated a new, more liberal social order that historian Hilary Hallett suggests instigated the revolution in social and sexual mores that swept the later half of the twentieth century. The Hollywood actress in particular modeled unprecedented sexual and professional independence both on and off the screen; actresses like Gloria Swanson emulated the sexually liberated, independent characters they played by divorcing without shame and refusing to let marriage and motherhood interfere with their careers.[34] One did not have to be a movie star to enjoy greater freedom and independence; even the working-class women who staffed the studio offices "lived happily like bachelors in the boomtowns of yore."[35] Enabled by their generous salaries, they emulated the latest in fashion and makeup, attended parties unchaperoned, and saw their new lifestyle reinforced night after night at the local movie theater.[36] In such a milieu, a woman like Bower—twice divorced and a single parent—enjoyed relief from the scrutiny that such women faced elsewhere. She also enjoyed professional opportunities that were opening up for women writers and directors in early Hollywood, who could help producers reach the women who dominated the market for movies at that time.[37] At her Glendale apartment, Bower could research her new novel and strengthen her ties with the movie business.

We know a few of the people who made up Bower's circle during this time, whose stories help flesh out the atmosphere of her new social world; Blanche Lovern and Goldie Colwell were "Tom Mix leading ladies" who were frequent guests at the Pocket ranch, along with cowboy actor Buck Connor.[38] Lovern, née Nessly, was the daughter of a settler family in Wichita, Kansas, who, on September 4, 1909, married cowboy Harry Lovern. Their story is an example of how intertwined ranching and show business had become. They were married on horseback in a wedding that was itself a glamorous western performance, reported in local newspapers: "The young folks were both reared on ranches, and it was simply their desire that they be married on horseback that led them to have the unique service. The groom was dressed in cowboy costume, with heavy chaps, a sombrero and riding boots. The bride rode astride her horse and was dressed in a handsome riding costume. Many people were attracted to the scene, as it became known during the day that Judge Mirick had been engaged to perform the service."[39]

By September 1912 Blanche was the first woman in Wichita to run a hardware store, but she did not remain in this occupation for long.[40] Perhaps she and Harry were among the young people influenced, a Kansas paper reported, "to leave their homes in the east and become cowboys through pictures of the '101' ranch which they had seen."[41] In any case, by May 1915 Harry was in the movie business and living in Glendale, and Blanche was planning to join him.[42] Few other traces of their existence survive, but we do know that Harry competed in at least one rodeo in Los Angeles and that Blanche was affiliated with the 101 Ranch, probably as a performer.[43] Blanche's name does not appear in connection with any silent films, which is not unusual for the early years of the industry when the studios resisted credit to any but their most famous performers.

Goldie Colwell and Buck Connor were also film actors. Kansas-born Colwell, according to IMDb, played mainly supporting roles in westerns and comedies. She and Bower became close during Bower's stay in Glendale.[44] A letter survives that reveals some details about Bower's relationship with Goldie and the lifestyle she led. Goldie had been dismissed from the Selig Polyscope Company in Glendale for her part in a car accident that involved a group of performers on a joyride. Los Angeles in the mid-teens teemed with "machines," and driving was as much a pastime as a means of transportation. In a letter to Selig Polyscope, advocating for her new friend, Bower reveals that she had spent much of the fall and winter of 1914–15 among the Glendale "bunch" and probably experienced her own share of joyrides through the Hollywood Hills. Bower believed that Goldie was wrongfully punished and tried to set the record straight with a letter to her employer:

> A story has been circulated that Goldie was one of a "souse party" as they are sometimes called. She would be very sorry to have you believe anything like that about her, because it is so far from the truth. She was riding home from the studio with Luella Maxan, Ed Gibson and Leo Maloney when the accident occurred. Leo refused to take them straight home, but chose to carry them around by Burbank in spite of their protests. The machine skidded and threw Goldie and Lou Maxan out. Both were hurt badly enough to make it impossible for them to work, though luckily there were no bones broken.
>
> I have been with the Glendale company a great deal this fall and winter, and have come to know the "bunch" intimately. I know Goldie well enough to be glad to count her among my very closest friends— which almost speaks for itself, doesn't it? She is not the kind who could be guilty of the things that are being said of her; I know from my own personal knowledge. She is as conscientious a worker as I have met, and I admire her very much both on the screen and in her private life.[45]

Another member of Bower's circle was cowboy actor Buck Connor, who claimed to be a former Texas Ranger, bronc rider, and performer in Wild West shows before launching his career as a moving picture actor and producer.[46] Bower's granddaughter would later investigate these claims and find no supporting documentation. The Texas Ranger Hall of Fame had no record of him, and its librarian suggested that he was among the many cowboy performers who "[laid] claim to having been a Texas Ranger as it added to the draw of the crowd."[47] During

Bower's winter in Los Angeles he and Bower began collaborating on Texas Ranger stories published in *The Popular* and *McClure's*, and Buck also consulted with Bower for her books on the film business.[48]

While Bower socialized with the Glendale "bunch" and worked on *Jean of the Lazy A*, Dele stayed at the Los Gatos boarding school, run by Lydia's new husband, Marvin Benson. Although Bower had chosen a school with familiar faces, Dele was miserable there, and for good reason.[49] It must have been difficult for a seven-year-old child who had recently become separated from her father to adjust to life without either parent.[50] Bower did not spend the Christmas holiday with her; instead she wrote a Christmas play for Dele's school pageant entitled "Santa Clause on Strike," with roles as "brownies and fairies" for the children to perform.[51] It was a "huge success," Dele later remembered.[52]

Possibly Bower did not spend Christmas with Dele because, as she wrote to Little, Brown in February, "I was taken very ill with a nervous breakdown to which I am subject." Bower's letter was to explain that the cleaning staff had accidentally thrown out the proofs of her latest novel, *The Flying U's Last Stand*. She had rented a house in the Hollywood Hills "where it is quiet" and planned to remain there for a few months. The house on Nichols Canyon Road—now a celebrity enclave—supplied a peaceful setting for Bower to finish *Jean of the Lazy A*.

Bower remained in the Hollywood Hills until July, missing the birth of Roy's child at the Pocket in April and racking up debts as she supported two households and continued to be "hampered with sickness."[53] Away from the mayhem of the movie colony, Bower completed *Jean of the Lazy A* before returning to the Pocket for the summer of 1915. The story of a "range girl to the last fiber of her being," *Jean of the Lazy A* inscribes what Bower learned about the film business during that winter in Los Angeles, while also returning to the Montana landscapes that had served her so well. Its eponymous heroine accidentally becomes a silent film star when she is discovered by a director filming on location at her Montana ranch. At first Jean is engaged as an anonymous stunt double, a job she takes on to earn money to save her ranch and get her father, who is wrongly convicted of murder, out of prison. However, she proves to be so talented that members of the film crew conspired to have her face revealed on camera so that the studio head could see her work. The plan succeeds, and Jean finds herself the star of a feature film called *Jean of the Lazy A*. When the film is completed, Jean is ushered to Los Angeles where, after a two-week vacation, she is to join the film studio as a lead actress; however, she accidentally stumbles upon a new lead in her father's case and spends her vacation exonerating him for the crime and getting their ranch back. The novel concludes with Jean quitting her studio job and returning to the ranch she loves.

Bower was aided in her depictions of the film industry by Buck Connor, who had become a close friend and collaborator. Bower considered Buck's input "an immense benefit . . . in painting the 'movie game' with absolute fidelity to realism."[54] In Buck Connor, Bower had found—or so she initially believed—a collaborator who, like Bertrand Sinclair, could give her access to a male-dominated space—in this case film production—that she could incorporate into her writing. In addition Buck agreed to act as Bower's "Motion Picture representative," giving her advice on promotional strategies and helping her secure film deals. In exchange Bower helped Buck become a published writer, using her influence at *The Popular* to publish several coauthored Texas Ranger stories over the winter and spring of 1914–15. In the fall of 1915, Buck drove with Bower to the Pocket, where the two narrowly escaped serious injury in a car accident when Bower's "machine turned a triple flip while descending a steep grade."[55] At the Pocket, they collaborated on another novel about western movie-making, this time featuring the famous Flying U cowboys, who delve into moving pictures when cowboy work dries up. *The Phantom Herd* transforms filmmaking into the stuff of western adventure as its protagonist, director Luck Lindsay, quits his comfortable studio job to make an epic western film, complete with a cattle roundup set during a blizzard. In one of her personal copies of *The Phantom Herd*, Bower wrote her memories of that September: "Another Pocket Ranch story written in the fall—crisp tangy air, the hillsides all gold and scarlet among the green."[56]

Bower's collaboration with Buck Connor, she believed, would strengthen her foothold in the film industry. In letters to Little, Brown, she expounded on Buck's ability to promote her books to film executives and tried to convince Little, Brown to grant him coauthorship on her film industry novels. At first her letters refer to him indirectly: "Through placing the motion picture rights of several of my stories, I have found it best to employ a business manager who is beginning a quiet publicity campaign which will do much to help increase my book sales. I am enclosing a card which is being sent out to several hundred addresses of those who would be interested."[57] Eventually Bower urged Little, Brown to give Buck equal billing as a coauthor of *The Phantom Herd*. "Aside from the justice of giving him credit for the work he does, his name will be of a certain value on a book. He is a very well-known motion picture producer, as well as Western character actor, and is acknowledged by the profession as an authority on Western technique."[58]

After wintering in Albuquerque, the setting for her new novel *The Heritage of the Sioux*—another film about western movie-making and a sequel to *The Phantom Herd*—Bower returned to the Pocket, where she and Buck assembled a collection of their Texas Ranger stories for book publication with Little, Brown. Again Bower pressed Little, Brown to list Buck as coauthor, suggesting that their collaboration had become a long-term arrangement:

> Buck Connor has a very wide acquaintance, and a following of his own in moving-picture circles, frontier shows and in Texas and the army. So, although he is unknown in literary work, his name is probably almost as widely known as my pen name; and it will bring a new following to our book trade. So far as one can predict the future I can say that we will be permanently associated in our work, and that there will be more stories of the Texas Rangers—unless a bit of lead should chance to put a stop to his activities down there at present, or some other untoward fate intervene. You could make some use, it seems to me, of the fact that he is a ranger himself—a very widely known one at that.[59]

Little, Brown was less enthusiastic about Bower's collaboration with Buck. Their letters seem irritated by her push for more Hollywood-style publicity campaigns and dismissive of her aspirations for closer ties with the film industry. To Bower's suggestion that they time her book publications with the release of the film version—now common practice—Little, Brown was lukewarm: "Except in the case of fifty cent books simultaneous motion picture production does not stimulate sales to any extent, and it is really not vital to us whether the story appears in motion pictures at the time of the publication or later."[60] For all of Bower's advocacy on Buck's behalf, Little, Brown considered him an imposition on the Bower brand. They limited his credit on *The Phantom Herd* to the preface and declined to publish the coauthored Texas Ranger book.[61] Nor were they supportive of Bower's interest in the budding film industry, still a relatively disreputable form. When Bower announced her plans for another book set in the film industry, Little, Brown was not enthusiastic: "We are inclined to think that your readers would prefer straight western drama to a story so permeated with moving picture atmosphere. While your new story as outlined promises well we hope that you will subordinate the motion picture part as we feel the best results can be obtained with stories of the same type as *The Ranch at the Wolverine* and *Lonesome Land*."[62]

By referencing these two books in particular, Little, Brown signaled their desire for Bower to leave the topic of filmmaking alone and return to writing about a West further removed from the modern world. For Bower, however, books about filming the West had provided the bridge she was looking for between the Montana cattle frontier that she had left behind and the more modern setting of California, which she had struggled to incorporate into her practice as a western writer. Bower had always been interested in a popular West that was part of the modern world, a theme that the emergent film industry enabled her to explore; her publishers, however, had other plans for her.

With her resources depleted, Bower decided that there would be no more traveling for the time being. Her film industry novels had not gone over well with either of her publishers—*The Popular* had even cut *The Phantom Herd* and *The Heritage of the Sioux* to single issues rather than serials, docking Bower's pay accordingly.[63] Bower had also dug herself into a financial hole through a pattern of trading long-term income from royalties for up-front cash payments to finance travel and the construction of the Pocket ranch. Making a virtue of necessity, Bower would settle down at the Pocket and set her next novel in the Plumas County area. She would also transform the Pocket into a productive ranch.

Putting the Pocket on a paying basis meant raising stock and crops that could help feed Bower's family and frequent guests while earning extra income for Bower. Trees would have to be cleared for farming, and the resulting lumber would be used to build a barn, fences, and other structures or sold to help pay for the equipment and workhorses needed to cultivate and harvest crops. These included hay, root vegetables, potatoes, and cabbage. A Jersey cow supplied milk for the household and perhaps some to sell. Fifteen Rhode Island Red chickens, seventy-five laying hens, and a beef cow provided meat and eggs.[64] An Irish laborer helped with the chores, often finding himself at odds with Bower's five purebred Airdales: "Trixie detests him, never will make friends with him and always wants to get at him if he goes near her. He has never harmed her at all—but I happen to know that he has a brutal streak in him toward dogs he does not like. I believe she senses and resents that brutality in his nature. Certain strangers she greets with wagglings and dog smiles, whereas she tried to tear the fence down if the choreman walks past the kennels."

This is a rare mention of the role of wage laborers in making the Pocket; Bower preferred to portray the ranch as her own singular achievement: "I am proud of the work I have done here; proud of the fact that a woman came into this valley and, with a wild pocket in the hills that had always been considered worthless except for hunting and fishing, made of it the most beautiful ranch in all of this country. Quincy is proud of The Pocket Ranch; proud to the point of being boastful—as I perhaps am."[65]

With Bower finally somewhat settled, Dele left the despised boarding school and reunited with her family. She enrolled in the local school in Quincy, California, impressing her peers with her larger-than-life mother. Years later, one of her old schoolmates remembered how Bower would drop Dele off at school in a horse and carriage. The children "would wait on the side of the road to watch, because [Bower] drove so fast." Another recalled how Bower would pick Dele up from school in an open touring car, making the other schoolchildren envious.[66]

At the Pocket, Bower surrounded herself with frequent houseguests and hosted dances and dinners for the community, warning her guests that formalities like "biled shirts and bar's grease are plum barred."[67] Buck Connor, who continued to coauthor Texas Ranger fiction with Bower, was still there, raising the eyebrows of neighbors who would later recall that "Bower had a cowboy with her at the Pocket ranch, and they used to give picnics in the yard and wear bandanas."[68] Lydia Benson and her baby daughter Jean were also there, as well as Bower's Hollywood friend Blanche Lovern. Lydia and Blanche were the guests of honor at a dance and midnight supper Bower held in September 1916 just as she was finishing *Starr, of the Desert*. More than forty guests were treated to a showing of Buck Connor's latest film in Quincy before reconvening at the Pocket, where signs in Bower's large living room admonished guests to "loosen up and be natural" as they danced "a mixture of quadrilles, Virginia reels, turkey-trots, [and] waltzes." Bower's player piano and gramophone alternated with live musicians to supply the music. Before the midnight supper, each guest was given "a rifle shell containing a piece of poetry which had been cut in half. The lady and gentleman whose pieces of poetry matched were supper partners, and a generous lunch done up in a red bandana handkerchief was presented to the gentleman. Inside this novel package was a lunch enclosed in a blue bandana for the lady."[69]

The convivial atmosphere at the Pocket was not to last. As the winter of 1916 progressed, the atmosphere became strained. Bower faced financial problems compounded by the expense of her growing household and another skirmish with her publishers. The quarrel was again between Bower's book and magazine publishers: Little, Brown had published *The Heritage of the Sioux* ahead of the serial publication in *The Popular*, infuriating Charles MacLean. The problem was compounded when MacLean discovered that *Jean of the Lazy A* had been published serially in a newspaper, violating his professed claim to all serial rights to Bower's work. Throughout the fall of 1916, a flurry of letters ranging in tone from terse to openly hostile were exchanged among Bower, MacLean, and Little, Brown vice president Alfred McIntyre, the upshot of which was that Bower lost her income for the serial publication of *The Heritage of the Sioux*. To prevent further financial embarrassment, Bower was forced to sell her latest book, *Starr, of the Desert*, for a reduced cash payment so that she could "tide things over."[70]

Meanwhile tensions arose among Bower and her many houseguests as the novelty of a "lodge in the wilderness" surrounded by friends and family gave way to the reality of confined spaces and clashing personalities. Things got bad enough that Bower did not speak to Lydia for the next four years, fell out with Blanche permanently, and "eased" Buck out of her life when she "found out that he was just using Bower to serve his own interests."[71] Letters and notes written years after the fact obliquely reveal the resentment that lingered long after the Pocket was sold, but they offer few details. In notes from the early 1920s, Bower disparages the same actors whose companionship she had sought during her time in Los Angeles: "They borrow their ideas and their habits. They have long waits between pictures. They don't read. They gossip and peddle scandal."[72] In her letter of reconciliation with Lydia, Bower remembered feeling alienated in her own home:

Kit was always yowling at Dele, and Dele was always scrapping with Jean, and Jean was always howling at you [Lydia.] And I know Blanche was mad because life was not one party after another, and blamed me for it, and Buck was making me write his stories and mine too and panning the whole bunch—but I thought I was coming through fairly well because I didn't go and hang myself to a tall pine tree (there being no weeping willows). . . . You and Blanche seemed to me to be lined up against me and would not talk when I was around, and that hurt, of course. But a good many things were also hurting about that time, and life looked pretty hard and unjust all around. I resented your turning to an outsider and being influenced against me.[73]

Decades later, in a terse exchange of letters with Dele, an aging Blanche would imply that something scandalous had gone on. It began when Dele, while researching her Bower biography, corresponded with Blanche about her memories of Bower. The exchange became hostile when Blanche claimed she was owed a Charles Russell painting that Bower had given her. At work on her own memoir, which she claimed was causing a "stir" with her publishers, Blanche threatened to reveal sensitive information about Bower.[74] We can only speculate about what Blanche had in mind; she may well have been alluding to Bower's relationship with Buck. However, her book never materialized, and the Russell painting had long ago been sold.

Bower's output since her return to the Pocket, spurred by financial difficulty, included *Starr, of the Desert*, her second New Mexico novel; *The Lookout Man*, her first novel set in Plumas County; and a road-trip novel entitled *Cabin Fever*. All of these works bridge the settings that Bower had become familiar with since moving to California, featuring urban Los Angelenos who are propelled by circumstance into some isolated western frontier—the New Mexico desert, the open road, a northern California forest fire lookout. Through the romance plots that Little, Brown demanded, Bower offered her characters resolutions to conflicts that evaded her in real life.

She found solace from financial and domestic difficulties in her growing passion for cars. She loved driving fast, knew basic automobile mechanics and maintenance, and was not afraid of traveling on extended trips with only her Airdale terrier for protection. Frustrated by her dependence on *The Popular*, she looked to the automobile as a means of diversifying her writing and finding new venues for her work. She outlined her plans in a letter to Little, Brown:

> I have planned a "circumtour" of these our United States. . . . I want the trip for my own pleasure and benefit. I want to write of the trip, as I go along; a series of articles written in a human, interested and interesting way. . . . I shall travel under the name B. M. Bower, and I shall have with me my little girl, a maid and my airdale dog, Barry. . . . I intend to keep a detailed diary of the trip for my own benefit. I do

not mean to make any record run at all. What I want to do is to travel comfortably and sensibly, stopping where the interest holds me, for a closer acquaintance with place or people[.] I mean to go with my eyes open to the possibilities of this country and to the real, intimate interests of each community. I may be all summer on the road, but I shall not mind that. There are so many points of view from which to take such a trip: Good roads, for instance, and the two I named, and my own personal experiences and adventure; whether it is practicable for a woman who is merely an ordinary, careful driver, to make a tour of that extent; the fun one would have, and the discouragement. There are so many different angles that I am studying now over those that will be of the most general interest.

The Airdale Barry was in training to guard Bower's car during the journey: "They can be taught to do anything except talk, and right now this three-months-old pup becomes frantic at the approach of a stranger, and will fight until exhausted, but never has given up. I don't believe he ever will. His mother is a killer by instinct, though very loyal and gentle with friends."[75]

In March 1917 a local newspaper announced Bower's purchase of a new Overland club car and reported her plans for a cross-country trip in search of material for a book.[76] It was an extravagant purchase for someone in the throes of a financial crisis, but Bower may well have received a favorable price in exchange for publicity for the Overland car company, which was mentioned in dozens of syndicated articles announcing that a famous author had purchased one of their cars. Bower's trip was not the one she had at first envisioned, however. Discouraged by Little, Brown from any projects that might divert her from writing their two novels a year and feeling pressure from her readers to return to the cowboy stories that had made her famous, Bower accepted an invitation from Frank Hastings of the sms Ranch to tour the famous Texas cattle operation. Hastings was hoping for the valuable publicity that an appearance in a Bower book would generate, and Bower saw an opportunity to reinvigorate her writing about the cattle frontier, telling McIntyre, "My readers seem to want it more than anything else. I do not mean to take up the Flying U, but build up an interest in another locality which I have in mind and which I have not yet touched upon. Modern life on a big cattle ranch should hold a fresh interest, as it has been little touched upon. I hope to prove that it is still picturesque, still touched with romance which the reading public demands."[77]

In June, Bower made the seven-day drive to the ranch, where, according to cattle buyer Ralph W. Selkirk, who also took the tour, she had "chuckwagon meals, talked with the boys, interviewed old timers, looked over the cattle and did everything that Mr. Hastings thought might interest the author." Selkirk's somewhat derogatory letter to *Montana: The Magazine of Western History* provides us with a taste of the sexism Bower must have experienced as a woman writing about male-dominated spaces and activities. He remembered her as reserved, "of medium height, rather stout and apparently not very interested in the people she met or in the things she was shown." Despite efforts by the sms Ranch to model itself after open range operations of yore, Selkirk—clearly unfamiliar with Bower's penchant for stories about the modern West—mused that its operations "were far different from the older days that she pictured in her stories and books. This may have accounted for lack of enthusiasm during her visit, [which] didn't produce any results for the ranch and evidently didn't give Mrs. Bower any usable ideas." Selkirk concludes with a nod to Bower's younger and prettier secretary, who accompanied her on the trip: "It was a thrill to spend several days in the same party with B. M. Bower, but I enjoyed the secretary more!"[78] For Bower's part, the trip was a chance for her to become reacquainted with working cowboys after her disappointing experience with Buck. On the back of one photo she took of the sms cowboys she wrote, "Real ones, who call Bower a friend."[79]

In August, Bower returned from Texas via Los Angeles, where she picked up Goldie Colwell—the one Hollywood friend she had not fallen out with—to accompany her back to the Pocket. At a time when long road trips were still a novelty, Bower's arrival in Quincy was noted in the local newspaper: "She drove her own car from Los Angeles to Quincy, a distance of 685 miles by way of the Coast route, in three and one half days, a feat of which anyone might well be proud."[80]

Whatever Bower's intentions were at that time, she would leave the Pocket for Los Angeles by the spring of 1918, never to return. Her decision seems to have been unplanned and followed a period in which Bower experienced considerable turmoil and made some radical choices. The trouble started on another trip to Los Angeles, where Roy had started a flight school in partnership with Joe Mattingly, who had gained notoriety as a stunt pilot. Roy had been fascinated by airplanes from childhood; Bower's investment in the aviation school was an extravagance that further demonstrated her favoritism toward Roy over her other children. In October, Bower left Goldie and her husband George Diegel as caretakers at the Pocket and drove to Los Angeles to visit Roy and Kitty. On that trip, a fall on the pavement left Bower with a seriously broken arm. The accident set her back in her work schedule—she was due to submit proofs to Little, Brown—and was also accompanied by a bout of "nervous prostration."[81] At around that time, Bower instructed Goldie and George to sell off much of the contents of the ranch. On October 11, Diegel advertised in the *Plumas National-Bulletin* the immediate sale of Bower's livestock, farm implements, feed, and other goods.[82] She may have needed quick cash, having been rendered unable to work; she may have decided to downsize without Roy to help run the Pocket. Whatever the case, Bower returned to the Pocket at the end of November, still unable to use her arm. She made yet another radical decision the following January to sell all of her remaining book rights. This may have been how Bower got the money to finance Roy's flight school. She told Little, Brown, however, that the money was to support the war effort.[83] "I have considered the sacrifice in future income and all that," she wrote to Little, Brown in January, "but still I want to do it. I am ready to earn for the future; but what I have done in the past must help in our common cause."[84]

In April 1918 Bower left Quincy for another visit with Roy, and this time she did not return. Local papers announced the sale of the Pocket in July.[85] Bower's former lodge in the wilderness changed hands again in 1920, when it was sold to an architect–interior designer duo who modernized the house with running water and a Delco-Light system.[86] In 1924 the fuel tank for that system exploded, destroying the house and all of its contents.[87]

1. Studio portrait of Newton (Chip) Muzzy and sister Bertha, aged ten and eleven, Minnesota, 1882. Courtesy B. M. Bower Papers, reprinted with the permission of Reed Doke.

2. Bertha and Clayton Bower, Montana, 1902. Courtesy B. M. Bower Papers, reprinted with the permission of Reed Doke.

3. Bertrand Sinclair, aka the "Fiddleback Kid," Big Sandy, Montana, circa 1902–3. Courtesy B. M. Bower Papers, reprinted with the permission of Reed Doke.

4. *Left to right*: Clayton, Harry, Roy, Bertha Grace, Bertha. Studio portrait taken while on vacation in Tacoma, Washington, circa 1902–3. Courtesy B. M. Bower Papers, reprinted with the permission of Reed Doke.

5. Bower at her typewriter, Big Sandy, Montana, 1904. Courtesy B. M. Bower Papers, reprinted with the permission of Reed Doke.

6. Bertrand Sinclair and B. M. Bower in front of Charles Russell's studio, 1906. Courtesy of Western History Collections, University of Oklahoma Libraries, Bertha Muzzy Bower Collection, image #31.

7. B. M. Bower's study in Santa Cruz, California, circa 1907–8. Courtesy of Western History Collections, University of Oklahoma Libraries, Bertha Muzzy Bower Collection, image #21.

8. Bower reading the *Encyclopædia Britannica* to daughter Della, aged two, summer camp, ca. 1909. Courtesy B. M. Bower Papers, reprinted with the permission of Reed Doke.

9. B. M. Bower writing *Lonesome Land*, summer camp, Carmel River, California, 1910. Courtesy of Western History Collections, University of Oklahoma Libraries, Bertha Muzzy Bower Collection, image #11.

10. Bower aiming her rifle, ca. 1909. Courtesy of Western History Collections, University of Oklahoma Libraries, Bertha Muzzy Bower Collection, image #12.

11. Bower with son Roy, 1912, taken after separation from Bertrand Sinclair. Courtesy B. M. Bower Papers, reprinted with the permission of Reed Doke.

12. Publicity photo, 1912. Courtesy B. M. Bower Papers, reprinted with the permission of Reed Doke.

13. Portrait of Bower, circa 1921. Courtesy B. M. Bower Papers, reprinted with the permission of Reed Doke.

4

Nature at Her Uncanny Worst

As the Great War ended, Bower's fame entered its peak. Her books had sold well despite the uncertainty of the war, and now sales surged, assisted by a deal Little, Brown had made with Grosset & Dunlap to capitalize on their acquisition of her copyrights and mass-produce cheap reprint editions of the Bower books. Little, Brown received daily inquiries from translators, foreign publishers, and film producers, all looking to get in on the Bower brand. Readers pitched story ideas and asked if it was true that Bower was a woman. Estranged family members and old friends wrote to inquire after Bower's whereabouts. Having sold her book rights to Little, Brown, who had lowballed its offer for them because of the uncertainty of wartime, Bower saw none of the multiplying profits of the postwar years, prompting a guilty-sounding McIntyre to send her a lump-sum payment of $1,000.[1] "Had we estimated correctly the probable condition of the fiction market in 1919, we should have made a more liberal offer," the publisher explained.[2] Bower acknowledged this unsolicited payment with gratitude: "I cannot haggle over money, and it is a real pleasure to me to know that I can be sure of fair treatment from you without it."[3] Although she had learned many lessons over the years about how to negotiate, the process was still uncomfortable for her.

Upon moving to Los Angeles, Bower threw herself into the local community of women writers and journalists, joining both the Women's Press Club and League of American Pen Women.[4] These groups, formed to offer women writers a space for professional development in the male-dominated fields of professional writing and journalism, were part of a thriving women's club movement that coincided with first-wave American feminism. Bower's alliance with women's organizations was a shift for her. A staunch individualist, she had never shown much interest in first-wave feminism despite witnessing the victory of woman suffrage in 1919. Although preferring plucky and opinionated heroines, she avoided feminist politics. But after a decade of being silenced by her publishers and losing out on much of the profit from her books, Bower sought out connections with other women writers and, despite renewed prohibitions from her publisher, delivered public talks as "B. M. Bower."[5] These activities raised her stature locally; she received more attention in the local press and joined such literary celebrities as Theodore Dreiser and Edgar Rice Burroughs at a prestigious literary dinner.[6] Little, Brown, however, had changed its position on publicizing Bower books and no longer included any images or biographical information that would reveal that B. M. Bower was a woman.

Bower's social activities involved spiritual, as well as professional, groups. Still writing at a furious pace, she began exploring faith-based healing practices to treat her bouts of ill health that became more frequent after the breakup of the Pocket and her move to Los Angeles. Christian Scientists gave regular public talks in Los Angeles while Bower lived there, and Bower's social circles also included practitioners of this relatively new religion, including Goldie Colwell, a Christian Science adherent.[7] The promise that bodily illnesses were illusions that could be healed through prayer offered relief from the chronic maladies that had plagued Bower for many years.

Among the old acquaintances who reached out to Bower during this period of rising fame was Robert "Bud" Cowan. Back in the early 1900s he had worked for McNamara and Marlow alongside Clayton Bower and Bertrand Sinclair. Although Bower's photo collection from those early days includes pictures of Bud showing off his roping skills, she didn't know him that well, only from community dances and musical evenings, where he sang and played multiple instruments.[8] Bud left Montana after the demand for cowboys declined and found work where he could, most recently running a freight business that had failed. Now living in Oakland, California, Bud could not help but notice Bower's name in bookstore windows and on magazine covers. He had even developed a notion that he was the inspiration for the original Chip, now famous thanks to the Tom Mix film version of Bower's first novel.[9] In August 1919 he wrote a letter to Little, Brown inquiring after Bower's whereabouts.[10] He had a proposition for her.

Bud's letter arrived just as Bower was preparing for a doctor-prescribed "sea voyage" to aid in her recovery from another illness that she and her doctors attributed to "severe strain." As she had done after previous major life crises, Bower immersed herself in her work after selling the Pocket. By the end of 1918 she had completed two novels— *Skyrider* and *The Thunder Bird*—both inspired by Roy's experiences in the navy as a member of the newly formed "Aviation Section." She had then spent January and February 1919 in Opid's Camp, a resort in Angeles National Forest, penning short fiction for *The Popular* for quick cash and, in response to pressure for more traditional western settings, conceptualizing a new long novel set back in "cow country."[11] In mid-May, shortly after her return to Los Angeles and while sending a telegram promising to have her new novel done by the end of June, she noticed feeling a bit sick. Before long, Bower was incapacitated by "a 'weak heart' caused by severe strain."[12] She wrote to Little, Brown to let them know the manuscript would be late and asked for an advance to pay for the "sea voyage."[13]

For the month of September 1919, the absence of any correspondence with her publisher or notations in her manuscript records suggests that Bower did indeed take some kind of vacation. Her papers contain few other details about the trip save that she planned to head "north," taking her in the direction of her favorite brother, Chip.[14] Compounding the mystery of Bower's whereabouts for September and October 1919 is what she did not long after returning to Los Angeles around October 21, 1919. In early November B. M. Bower and Bud Cowan took out a marriage license in Santa Ana, California—only two months (roughly) after Bud had written to Little, Brown.[15] Either the two had reconnected and had a whirlwind romance in the two weeks following Bower's return from her mysterious sea voyage, or the voyage itself had something to do with their courtship. In any case, Bud, along with his teenage son, was soon installed in the Bower household, along with Roy, Kitty, their son Roy Jr., and Bower's older sister Kate Muzzy. When the census takers came to their door in January 1920, they reported Bower as a widow and Cowan as her boarder.[16] Bower did not disclose her marriage to Little, Brown for another two years.[17]

Bower embarked on a number of initiatives in late 1919 and early 1920, including a new book contract with Little, Brown, renewed efforts in the film business, and, influenced by Bud's entry into her life, a return in her writing to the "cow country" theme that had made her famous in the first place. She also vowed to take better care of her health, prompted by her most recent illness. She made sure her new book contract with Little, Brown did not hold her to inflexible deadlines, promising Little, Brown that the result would be better quality fiction. "I cannot drive myself as I once did," she explained in a letter to her publisher. "I can no longer force myself to write under nervous strain. My nerves will no longer bear any extra strain. Complete exhaustion follows the spur."[18] Bower's return to film work involved Benjamin Hampton of the newly formed Great Authors Pictures Inc., which specialized in film versions of well-known novels and was scheduled to produce her latest novel, *Rim o' the World*, in the spring. These efforts were hampered somewhat by the fact that Bower had sold out her book rights, a choice she now regretted and was even embarrassed about. She asked McIntyre, in his dealings with Hampton, not to disclose that Little, Brown owned her book rights:

> There is a great deal of camouflage in the picture production, and I do not want Mr. Hampton to know that I have sold out my book rights. He seems to think that book royalties run into the tens of thousands each year, and I have no desire to undeceive him. It seems to be the way the game is played in pictures. Incomes are so inflated—and one's value is rated solely by the advertised number of dollars. He would be shocked to know that one of his "Great Authors" found it convenient to sell her book rights.[19]

Little, Brown indulged Bower's side projects for so long before steering her back to writing cowboy fiction even though the subject was starting to bore her. In this respect, Bud's arrival was opportune, providing Bower with fresh western subject matter. Unlike Bower—who had embraced the modern world and loved driving, the movies, and the social opportunities of the city—Bud never could let go of his cowpuncher days and was more than happy to serve as the basis for a new Bower book.[20] His story, Bower promised her publishers, was just the thing to counter misleading representations of the West in the increasingly popular movie westerns:

> [It] will, I hope, give a true and a vivid picture of the *real* West, from the time when the first trail herds went North from Texas. I have absolutely authentic data upon which to base the earlier part, and am starting my leading character as a child being taken by his parents from Texas to Wyoming with a trail herd. I want to show what a real Western-bred man is like. Too often have they been pictured of the Alkali Ike type, or the Wild Bill brand of desperado. The movies have almost submerged the real Western character.[21]

Bower would later admit that she also wrote *Cow-Country* to placate Bud when he found out that he had not been the model for her most famous cowboy. "It was to console Bud for *not* being 'the original Chip' that I wrote *Cow-Country* around and for him."[22]

Bud's arrival in Bower's life brought about one other profound change: he had gotten wind of the location of a fabled lost mine in Nevada, and he wanted Bower to invest. The scheme appealed to her, as she later told Little, Brown, on two fronts:

> A fortune in money, and a lot of new, first-hand material for stories. . . . It seems a bit strange that a writer of fiction should stumble upon a chance to help locate a "lost" mine known all through the West. In Montana, twenty years ago, I heard of "The Captain Jack" lost mine. Now I have it located, and the whole story would make a

book without any professional frills. . . . [The man who found it] has already had a non-fatal gun fight over it, and a group of Tonopak mining men are itching to get hold of it. It's really almost melodramatic, besides the money value.[23]

Bower believed that the mine was the object of a local legend—a lost Mexican mine that, some fifty years earlier, had produced large amounts of silver before the men working the mine were hanged for horse stealing and the mine's location was lost.[24] Told by a mining engineer that the mine was rich in lead, copper, and silver, Bower acted quickly to procure it before someone else could. So convinced was Bower of the promise of the mine that, against Little, Brown's advice, she continued to sell her book rights up front so that she could develop her mine without outside investors and purchase the claims adjacent to her own.[25] In hindsight Bower's choices seem reckless, but she did consult various "experts" over the course of her venture who encouraged her to continue.[26] It took an extensive search to find the owner of the claims she wanted to buy. Ralph N. Early, a wealthy Pasadenan, sold her the claim for one hundred dollars and a position as secretary and treasurer of Bower's new mining company, which she named El Picacho Mine.[27]

Such tales of lost mines in the desert had circulated since at least the nineteenth century. Not long after Bud told Bower about his lost mine, Texas folklorist J. Frank Dobie compiled an anthology of similar stories titled *Coronado's Children* (1930).[28] A legendary mine in the desert struck Bower—however naïvely—as an ideal atmosphere for writing, something she hadn't had since the demise of the Pocket. The corresponding chance to strike it rich and finally overcome the financial deficits that had plagued her for most of her life made the prospect irresistible. For the next two years, she divided her time between Los Angeles and Las Vegas, Nevada, writing short fiction for *The Popular* to make ends meet, while she negotiated the acquisition of mining claims and oversaw the formation of a mining company.

On her frequent trips to Nevada, Bower continued to gather material for her fiction while she developed her mining company. No other environment except Montana had inspired Bower as much as Nevada.

"The whole country here is steeped in weird, sinister, romantic atmosphere," she wrote to her editor.[29] It "combines cattle and mines in the same localities and furnishes withal the sinister element of the desert."[30] The desert, Bower maintained, was "nature at her uncanny worst."[31] Avoiding lengthy novels while she focused on the mine, Bower developed a new character for short fiction that she could write quickly for *The Popular*: Casey Ryan, a former stage driver put out of business by the automobile, who stumbles from scheme to scheme to make a living in a modernizing desert west.

The mine rapidly became Bower's main hope for securing her future as her other projects, for various reasons, fell by the wayside. She saw little income from film deals, so she ended her contract with Ben Hampton after he failed to fulfill his promises of lavish productions of her novels.[32] *The Ranch at the Wolverine* avoided a similar fate; its distributor "wanted the picture cut down to bare plot action, leaving out some very beautiful character and atmosphere stuff, and bringing it down to the cheap release idea of a Western picture." The film's producer, however, shared Bower's point of view. After *Wolverine* was released with a new distributor, Bower received positive reports of its success, although her income from film rights was negligible.[33]

Meanwhile Bower's writing income, already suffering from lower productivity and the up-front sale of her book rights, was compromised even further when Charles MacLean at *The Popular* published *Cow-Country* in one issue—knowing full well that Little, Brown would object—and took advantage of the fact that Bower had failed to specify any restrictions in her contract for the work. Predicting lost sales as a result, Little, Brown cut their advance payment to Bower. Hoping to put the problem of single-issue publications in *The Popular* to bed once and for all, Bower wrote to MacLean with strict instructions that her works were never to be published in one issue.[34]

Although Bower had promised Little, Brown that mining would give her ideas for more stories, she soon found she could not juggle them both. After she became ill again in the summer of 1921, she wrote apologetically to Little, Brown to tell them that her next novel would have to wait. "[Writing and mining] are great games, both of them," she wrote to McIntyre. "I'd love to play the two as a duet—which is a mixed metaphor but nevertheless expresses my heart's desire. But I know that I must play one at a time or fail in both." Convinced by "experts" that her mine was destined to make her rich, Bower chose to focus on the mine. "It is worthwhile for the thing promises to yield a real fortune that may run into millions."[35]

By February 1922 Bower and Bud had fired Ralph Early for misman-agement and moved to the mine permanently.[36] El Picacho Mine was nestled at the foot of a desert mountain range in Nye County, about 125 miles from Las Vegas. At that time, the surrounding canyon was home to quail, lynx, bobcats, and mountain sheep, but it is now part of the Nevada Test Site. Aside from Bower's stone writing cabin—the sturdiest edifice at El Picacho—the camp consisted of an improvised collection of small cabins, tents, a cookhouse, a makeshift garage, a chicken yard, and a large cistern for water.[37] They relied heavily on canned food purchased in Las Vegas during their twice-monthly road trips to the city for mail and supplies. A 1996 archeological survey of the site found extensive discarded cans that had once contained lard, milk, fruit, vegetables, and meat.[38] Fresh meat was a rare treat reserved for holidays, when they slaughtered a turkey reserved for that purpose, or when Bud was able to bring home some game. Water had to be hauled in and was precious. Any water that they didn't drink was recycled: washing water was used to clean the dishes; used dishwater was used to scrub the floor.[39] Like Bower's previous "camps," El Picacho pos-sessed a few domestic comforts, such as an improvised stone terrace outside, homemade curtains for the cabins to shield occupants from the desert sun, an extensive book collection, and a new radio. In the evenings Bower and Bud would scan the radio for concert broadcasts from San Francisco, Los Angeles, and Portland. "You can't realize what a difference it makes to sit in the evening and listen to music from all up and down the coast."[40]

Living at the mine were Bower, Bud, Roy, a cook, and, when they could afford to pay them, several hired men. A suite of relatives came and went to visit or help out with the mine, including Chip's son Elmer Muzzy, who was Roy's age; Bud's daughter, Martha Sheahan, and her husband, Dan; and Bower's niece Agnes Johnson, daughter of Bower's sister Vine. During holidays they were joined by Dele, who attended high school in Los Angeles. "We live a life that is as quiet as that in a New England village," Bower said of the life at the camp. "Occasionally a prospector with burros stumbles in and brings a little color."[41] Bower liked showing the operation to visitors; they could be seen approaching from far away, which gave the cook enough time to prepare a welcome meal for them. The camp was sometimes also visited by members of the Western Shoshone tribes, whose traditional territory included Nye County.[42] A pet parrot named Polly provided additional company and was also recruited as a character in Bower's novel *The Parowan Bonanza*, but its vocal antics became more of an irritant than anything, so the parrot was rehomed with Bud's daughter.[43]

Another visitor to the camp was an avid Bower fan and aspiring writer named Paul Eldredge, who, upon learning of Bower's mining venture from the newspapers, made the trek to the mine. After a day's drive through the desert, Eldredge reached his destination. This is how he later described his arrival: "A group of buildings. A shaft in the side of the mountain. In front of one of the one-story buildings a big man in a gray Stetson hat who dwarfed a sturdy almost stocky woman with a green eye shade slanted over her forehead stood as if waiting for us, though actually it was to make out the identity of the unprecedented invasion, for this was the end of the trail."[44] Warmly received at the camp, Eldredge ended up living there for several weeks, becoming fully integrated into camp life:

> While I'd been there I'd told Bower that I had a story I wanted to write. She suggested I write it. It seemed better, however, to pitch horseshoes with Dele; to join in the camp singing under the stars after supper, Bud picking his mandolin; to help Bud muck out—all too infrequently, I'm sure—when he blasted closer to the ore vein in the side of the mountain; to peel a few spuds with the cook and hark to his talks. I think we went over to the Groom mine [a neighboring mine] too, the cook and Dele and I, and consorted with the young people there a couple of times while Bud blasted and Bower wrote.[45]

Despite plans to focus on the mine full-time, by 1922 Bower had to write constantly to keep the mine afloat. Every morning she "[trudged] up to her separate cabin . . . , the inevitable green eye-shade slanted over her forehead."[46] Most days her writing table was piled high with work, from galleys to correct to mining paperwork to complete. She wrote under the watchful eye of Alfred McIntyre and his colleagues at Little, Brown, whose portraits gazed upon her from the pages of a Little, Brown brochure that she had attached to the wall.[47] After a day of writing by the cabin window, she reemerged "as regularly as a factory hand released by the whistle, a sheaf of typed pages in her hand."[48] During evenings around the campfire Bower would test her work on the members of the camp, who she considered a highly representative readership comprising impressionable youth, the workers whose livelihood she depicted, and seasoned literary critics:

> Here in camp, everyone insists upon hearing my stories read as I go along, chapter by chapter. They are a wideawake, critical audience, I assure you. The miners, my family, everyone gathers eagerly to listen to "Bower" readings. My mining camp stuff must pass the critical mind of the men who have mined all their lives and followed boom after boom. My desert must line up with reality. Not a paragraph could slip through unchallenged. . . . I consider the reading public well represented here, for my listeners range from two high school students—a boy and a girl—through the miners and so to two or three who are really capable of judging literary quality.[49]

Even under the duress of a punishing writing schedule, Bower found the Nevada desert rich fodder for stories and was optimistic about the writing she produced there. She hired an agent to place her magazine fiction, hoping to branch out from *The Popular* and gain a foothold in the more prestigious slick magazines. In early 1922 Bower completed a novel featuring her popular Casey Ryan character and made plans for a new novel about bootlegging, also set in the desert, called *Desert Brew*. She had begun dictating her novels to Agnes, which she felt saved her tremendous time and energy.[50] However, McIntyre expressed skepticism that this new practice would yield quality manuscripts: "I shall be much interested in seeing how smoothly it reads, in view of the fact that it was dictated directly to the typewriter and has had no revision. You must have had your plot and your characters very clearly in your mind to be able to accomplish this."[51] According to family members, Bower did have an uncanny ability to develop stories and characters thoroughly in her mind before committing them to paper.[52]

Although she had no shortage of story ideas, the same could not be said of Bower's finances. She could barely write fast enough to keep her family fed and the mine operating. As her book sales surged and she saw none of the profits, she deeply regretted the sale of her copyrights and inquired with Little, Brown about the possibility of buying them back: "Mr. McIntyre, I have never felt happy over the sale of my copyrights. That I was forced to sell them was a sacrifice made for sake of other things which seemed to me worthy the cause. Now, by stretching a point I believe that I can buy them back and let you publish them under royalty plan as before."[53] McIntyre refused, citing the investments Little, Brown had made in her copyrights, including reprint deals with other publishers, and he scolded her for thinking such a thing was possible: "You will recollect that we have always advised you against disposing of these copyrights, and have pointed out to you that in the end you would lose by so doing."[54] In fact Little, Brown had *not* warned her that the sale of her book rights was final. "I did not realize it would be such a complicated transaction," Bower replied. "I thought that I could, for a fair price, return to the royalty basis."[55] Her farming background had taught her to view the sale of her copyrights as reversible, like that of a horse or a plot of land. That principle, she realized too late, did not apply in the more nebulous world of book publishing.

The issue of publicity emerged as another bone of contention between Bower and Little, Brown. After the publication of *The Gringos* in 1913, the publisher stopped publicizing Bower's identity—although they truthfully answered letters from curious readers, who occasionally wrote in to ask about Bower's sex. It is not clear from extant records why the publisher changed its policy. Sales of *The Gringos* had dipped, but that had originally been blamed on competition from Dilling-ham, who advertised their Bower book at about the same time that *The Gringos* was published. The acquisition of Bower's copyrights and reprint deal with Grosset & Dunlap may have motivated Little, Brown to exert more control over the Bower brand. Finally Zane Grey had come on the scene; his first western stories were published in 1911, and he was considered Bower's main rival.[56] His macho image and more violent, male-centered brand of western was making its mark on the genre, perhaps contributing to McIntyre's increasing anxiety about Bower's gender.

Bower, however, had been receiving considerable attention from southwestern newspapers, especially in California and Nevada, because of her mining venture. They marveled that the author of the famous Bower books was not only a woman but also the president of a min-ing company. "Author Shops for Dynamite," read a headline in the *Los Angeles Times*, next to a large portrait of Bower.[57] Her participation in women's organizations in both Los Angeles and Las Vegas also brought increased public exposure, which may well have demonstrated that her gender was not the scandal her publishers warned her about.[58] So she broached the topic with McIntyre: "My active work in developing a new mining district has resulted in creating a spontaneous kind of publicity which has opened the way to a dignified, perfectly legiti-mate direction of the public's interest through recognized channels. The fact that I am a woman and the author of many Western books lends a certain glamor, it appears, to the pioneer work I have done for the past year. That I am the only woman who is president and general manager of a mining corporation seems to have caught the attention of the general public."[59]

McIntyre replied with strong opposition while also rewriting history, conveniently forgetting Little, Brown's early publicity of Bower's identity: "It has been our experience that readers of Western stories are apt to be prejudiced against those which they know to be the work of a woman and we have always been careful to say nothing at all about the sex of B. M. Bower. I realize that a certain number of people know of it, but I am confident that the general public does not, and I am inclined to think that any publicity which comes from the dissemination of this information is apt to be undesirable."[60] It's questionable that McIntyre had much evidence for his position. Several other female writers, including Caroline Lockhart, Vingie Roe, and Katharine Newlin Burt, were also enjoying success as western novelists without concealing their gender. Moreover, Little, Brown occasionally fielded letters from curious readers who had heard the rumor that B. M. Bower was a woman, none of which hinted at anything scandalous. For example, Edith V. Anderson, a reader from Minneapolis, wrote:

> I have heard many discussions among people who have read B. M. Bower's books as to who the author really is; some say these books are written by a man and some have heard that B. M. Bower is a woman, others think that all of these books were not written by the same person. . . . Could you settle this question for us and also give a little information as to where he or she lives, etc? I would appreciate this very much as I have read almost every one of the books written by B. M. Bower and am very much interested in them.[61]

The possibility that Bower was a woman, Anderson's letter suggests, piqued readers' interest and actually enhanced the Bower brand. This had been Bower's own experience when readers learned of her identity, as she explained in her reply to McIntyre:

> I have discovered an invariable increase of interest in the part of readers who learn that "Bower" is a woman. The women are proud of the fact that another woman has succeeded in "putting one over" on the men. While the men seemed tickled to think that a woman could fool them so long. . . . B. M. Bower, after seventeen years of continuous writing, will lose nothing by the disclosure of her sex. When you first published my photograph and revealed my identity I was a bit fearful of the result. But in all the ten years I have known of just one man who was unhappily affected by the disclosure. He was an Englishman who had been a most enthusiastic Bower fan, and he deeply resented the fact that he had actually failed to discover

from my writings that I was a woman. . . . He is the one exception. Wherever I have gone, whether it be city, desert or range country, men and women have gone hunting Bower books immediately upon discovering Bower's real identity. Since this mine venture has brought my name before the public I have received many letters from strangers who seem glad to know B. M. Bower is a woman.[62]

This was Bower's most forceful letter yet on the subject of her public identity, but its civil tone obscures her frustration, which she expressed in a rare, private note that survives from the period: "[B. M. Bower] is a freak in not being a freak."[63]

McIntyre relented only enough to consult his head salesman on the matter. Dismissing Bower's argument that her identity as a woman was already well-known, McIntyre quoted his head salesman's response: "It is a mistake to advertise the fact that B. M. Bower is a woman, and I hope you will not advertise this fact to the buying public, especially in the West. I feel positive it will have an unfavorable result. The big trade know she is writing under a nom-de-plume, but they do not advertise this fact to the public."[64] There is no evidence in their archives that Little, Brown's sales department based its advice on sales figures, surveys, or other quantitative analyses.

As the author churned out more material to support the mine, her editor feared that Bower's renewed productivity was compromising the quality of her writing. He was not keen on much of her subject matter, and he questioned some of her aesthetic choices. He continued to press Bower for more stories about a mythical West of the open range, wilderness, and cowboys, whereas Bower was interested in modern topics like mining corporations, bootlegging, and industrial development. Bower's letters of 1922 hint at impatience with both McIntyre's criticism and his lack of understanding of the American West. She repeatedly reminded him that she was "living" the stories she was writing and knew her readers better than McIntyre did. On receipt of a new manuscript in May, McIntyre hinted that the quality of her work was slipping and that he preferred she return to writing the cowboy novels for which she was most well-known: "[*The Voice at Johnnywater*] does not appeal to me as having the strength of *Cow-Country* or two or three other of your novels. You must be working more rapidly than in the past, for I judge that you have written *The Voice at Johnnywater* in five or six weeks."[65] Bower defended her experimentation with western subject matter: "In writing a great number of novels, it seems to me vital that an author should avoid that killing quality of sameness. I have tried to have the last story always different from preceding ones."[66] She submitted another new manuscript for her novel about the Colorado River (Hoover) dam some three months later, touting it as having "a significance quite apart from its story value." She continued, "I hope that I shall never be guilty of writing a propaganda story. But it happens that the damming of the Colorado has become a subject of national importance and interest, so that the book is a timely one."[67] McIntyre was lukewarm on the subject matter and harsh about the quality: "I don't think you have taken as long as usual to write either this story or *The Voice at Johnnywater*, and I cannot help feeling both stories have suffered in consequence. Both manuscripts show frequent errors in spelling and punctuation, which indicate that they have not received any revision at your hands."[68] Bower defended the manuscript, suggesting that Little, Brown's new proofreader was applying a new style to which she was unaccustomed while asserting that her new story had received the approval of "men who are in close touch with the reclamation of the Colorado River"—a subject the white-collar Bostonian McIntyre, Bower hinted, knew little about.[69] Upon submitting her third manuscript of 1922, Bower anticipated and challenged McIntyre's criticism that she was once again rushing the job:

Under separate cover, I am enclosing the manuscript of my last novel under the contract, *Parowan*. I had all these novel plots in my mind during the year and more when I was not writing at all, so this year, with everything favorable for uninterrupted work, I have done them all. They are not really just thrown together. "Johnnywater" plot is three years old, you remember. "The Eagle's Wing" has been brewing since away last winter—and this *Parowan* story I have had in synopsis form for a year and a half. I am telling you this because you have thought that I am writing too fast. I have merely been putting on paper stories with which I have been living intimately for a long while. I wonder if you will observe that I have achieved a mining story without burning a lot of gunpowder? Now that I have spent so much time in the desert, I have discovered that even a boom need not be classed as "extra-hazardous" in fiction. I feel like a pioneer in this, and I think you should proceed at once to put me in my place again, lest I forget the importance of modesty as a cardinal virtue.[70]

The last line in particular is a subtle but unmistakable criticism of McIntyre's controlling editorial style, as well as a defense of Bower's authorial integrity.

Repeatedly throughout these exchanges, Bower also asserts her authority over her subject matter as someone who, unlike her Bostonian publishers, lives in the western spaces she is writing about. When McIntyre complained about technical problems with the *Parowan* manuscript, Bower again reminded him that he had little grasp of the world whose fictional representation he was gatekeeping:

I wonder if you realize just what it means to be a hundred-and-twenty miles from a post office, with desert roads to traverse. From now until spring we must run the gauntlet of storms as well. There is a long valley, an extinct crater, really, which contains the "red lake"—a bald twelve miles of lava silt that becomes a mass of glue when it is wet. To "hit the red lake in a storm" means hardships, adventure, the drawing upon all our mental and physical resources to overcome the obstacle. So forgive the missing page, will you, and the duplicate?[71]

Bower also defended her manuscript against McIntyre's critique of her plot. The more conservative McIntyre found implausible the sudden rise and fall of the fortunes of her protagonist, a prospector named

Hopeful Bill, who, after a lifetime of searching, strikes it rich, only to lose his fortune to his crooked business partner. To save his mine and his reputation, he buys back all of his stock, installs himself at the mine, and brings it back to prosperity, this time as a small, family-run operation. Bower defended her story by once more reminding McIntyre, although not in so many words, that he did not know what he was talking about: "I assure you that fortunes are made easily in a year, in oil and in mines," she asserted. "I could write you a book of facts which would seem more like fiction than does *Parowan*. El Picacho Mine will have—is making—a history that will make melodramatic reading, I assure you."[72] McIntyre also wanted Bower to depict the protagonist's strained relationship with his wife more explicitly by representing her point of view, which Bower also objected would compromise her realism: "I [do] not read the minds of the others for the readers' benefit. So many have asked me how I make my people seem real, and while I am not sure, I think perhaps that is one way in which it is done. I live one character throughout the story." Bower was not the only one who believed in the manuscript as she wrote it. Herbert Jenkins, director of Little, Brown's publishing department, thought *The Parowan Bonanza* to be one of Bower's best novels.[73]

Bower's defense of *The Parowan Bonanza* also describes her own resolve as she poured virtually all of her income into El Picacho Mine, convinced that it would yield its own "bonanza":

I firmly believe in destiny and a law that governs the lives of men. In my own experience I have found it so. An emergency such as Bill faced *could* be met. It always can if one does not shirk the problem. It is astonishing how closely "fate" sometimes figures one's needs down to the last dollar, the last pound of bacon, the last ounce of energy. I am writing, these days, of life as I know it—not of life as other writers write it. . . . [Bill's] faith and his strength of purpose would be tested to the limit, to prove whether he was worthy of a greater success. It is so. I know it. I am proving that principle nearly every day, right here in the pioneer work to which I am dedicated.[74]

At the end of *The Parowan Bonanza*, Bower's protagonist is rewarded when he discovers a new vein rich enough to support his family on a modest but sustainable scale. This was precisely the outcome that Bower hoped for El Picacho. The teachings of Christian Science are evident in her explanation of Bill's and her own capacity to determine the future through "faith" and "strength of purpose."

Despite Bower's earlier regrets for selling her royalty rights in exchange for quick cash from Little, Brown, she resumed the practice in early 1923 in order to invest in the mine, still convinced that it was about to pay off. Doing so, she explained to Little, Brown, "not only promises greater returns but . . . will benefit a greater number of persons than if I had clung to my royalties."[75] At the time, she viewed this arrangement as temporary. "We are hoping that this summer and fall will see our work brought to a successful conclusion and since I have gained much in health and in fresh material for future work, the small sacrifice should not be regretted."[76] She supplemented this advance by writing periodical fiction for quick cash, writing only one novel in 1923.[77]

The summer of 1923 came and went, and still there was no big payoff from the mine. By November money had almost run out, and periodical writing had not been as lucrative as Bower hoped. Bower's only prospect was her next novel *Desert Brew*, which was not scheduled for publication until the spring of 1925. In her letter asking Little, Brown for payment a full year in advance, Bower argued that the money would be a good investment: "This high-pressure game we are playing with these desert hills should mean better stories, written with a keener insight into the wilderness and its people. I feel sure that we shall win—and then, no more pioneering except on paper. In the meantime the fight is good and clean and we shall make a good many persons happier and more prosperous by winning. So it is surely worthwhile."[78] Little, Brown reluctantly issued the advance, docking Bower one hundred dollars in interest from the three-thousand-dollar-advance payment and bearing more bad news for Bower's prospects as Christmas approached: Bower's sales were slipping.[79]

Bower's reply to Little, Brown some two weeks later continues to insist on the value of the mine, but the note of desperation is unmistakable:

"With a really valuable property here, and with our names standing at the head of the enterprise, we simply must carry on as a matter of self respect. We cannot let go and see any stockholder suffer loss while it is humanly possible to go on. Neither can we offer the public any stock and be looked at askance as possible wild-catters. We are in something of the same position as Hopeful Bill when he bought up the Parowan stock."[80]

They worked at the mine through Christmas rather than spending the holiday in Las Vegas, blasting until the powder ran out without finding anything but encouraged to continue by a positive engineering report, as well as Bower's religious practices.[81] By applying the teachings of Christian Science and the Unity School of Christianity, Bower hoped for physical and mental healing. She believed that these efforts were working: "To be sure, I haven't had enough money to go around, but I have made many other demonstrations of healing and harmony and protection, and the demonstrations of prosperity are beginning to show forth." Among these "demonstrations of prosperity" was a possible windfall for Bud: "I believe that the knowledge came through my Unity work, as a demonstration; therefore I believe it is coming to pass. A second cousin (making it brief) died intestate and left over $14,000,000 and no heirs. For four years they have been hunting for the next of kin, and the administrator, seeing Jimmie's [Bud's brother Jimmie Cowan] picture in the LA paper, wrote saying that the resemblance to the deceased was so strong that he felt Jimmie must be a relative."[82]

The new year saw no progress at the mine, and with reports of slipping sales, Bower began work on "a range story of the old type," hoping, she wrote Little, Brown, to replicate the success of her early Montana books: "I am creating another Happy Family, I hope. There will be short stories of the Meadowlark [cowboys] appearing from time to time in magazines, and I hope that will increase the sales of the book for you."[83] Bower continued to sell her book rights up front and pressed for early payments, but this time there was no mention of any imminent mining bonanza, only veiled and terse telegrammed apologies: "sorry to do this at this time but unavoidable."[84] Little, Brown was highly critical of the first manuscript in Bower's proposed new Montana series, which was doubtless written under the duress of the mine's poor performance, Bower's growing estrangement from Montana, as well as the sudden appearance in Bower's life of a ghost from her past.[85]

That ghost was Harry Bower, Bower's oldest son, whom she had not seen since their brief reunion at the Carmel writing camp in 1910. Nor had she told her publishers about the existence of an estranged son from her first marriage. Harry had just returned to the United States after spending several difficult years in Australia, where his sister, Bertha Grace, had emigrated. Most of this time was spent serving two prison sentences for robbery before enlisting with the Australian military—he lied on his application that he was a Canadian citizen with no criminal record.[86] After making his way back to the United States, Harry decided to track down his mother. He wrote to Little, Brown in May 1924 a rambling but poignant letter asking them for his mother's address and giving the publisher a glimpse into a private life that Bower had preferred to keep to herself. It broke his heart, Harry wrote, to see Bower's books everywhere yet not know where she lived. He verified his identity by offering details about Bower's past—such as the names of the pack mules purchased for their summer camps in Carmel—and asked the publisher if a story from the famous writer's son would interest them.[87]

Coming on the heels of the failure of the mine to yield the bonanza Bower had predicted, Harry's letter threatened to further damage her professional reputation with her publisher; in the early twentieth century, family breakups were regarded as a mark of moral failure, particularly on the part of mothers. Bower immediately wrote Little, Brown a letter of explanation. In it she painted Harry as a drifter after her money, such as it was, and she misrepresented her part in their estrangement:

> His letter to you speaks for itself, and reveals the one great sorrow in my rather sorrowful life. Harold left home when he was a boy and rebelled against school, went to Australia, from there to other countries—who will ever know the true history of a youth who is by choice a drifter? I suppose letters sent to my old address failed to

reach me and he has taken this method of getting in touch. I should be very happy to hear from him—but I can find no evidence of any change for the better—no hope that he even wants to change. His letter to me is merely a reproach that I have not answered other letters in which he says he asked for money. I am sorry that this personal trouble of mine has been forced upon the attention of my publishers, and I feel that you are entitled to this explanation from me. I am neither hard, selfish nor without maternal affection, but sometimes I am made to appear all of these unlovely things.[88]

As Bower navigated Harry's return to her life, things at the mine grew no better. In June 1924 she and Bud trekked north to Reno, Nevada, explaining to the local newspaper that "Bud grew a little lonesome out there" at the mine.[89] The reality was that the mine had still not produced an ounce of silver, and Bower would never return to camp. The trip to Reno may have been more than just a vacation. While in the area, Bower and Bud had lunch with Nevada governor J. G. "Scruggs" Scrugham in Carson City, and not long afterward, both of them had government positions: Bud became chief of police in Las Vegas despite having no previous law enforcement experience, and Bower was appointed to a "board of historical research" established by the governor.[90] By the fall of 1924 Bower, Bud, Roy, and Dele had moved to Las Vegas.

The hoped-for inheritance hadn't materialized either—nor would it. In 1926 Bud would advertise a $50,000 reward for the return of a family Bible that, he claimed, proved his relation to the late oil millionaire William P. Cowan.[91] This last-ditch effort would come to nothing. To make ends meet, Bower wrote a steady stream of short fiction that she now handled herself, having fired her literary agency for its disappointing performance. Still hoping to broaden her presence beyond The Popular, she submitted to its competitor Short Stories, published by Doubleday, as well as more slick magazines like the Saturday Evening Post and Collier's.

After she left the mine, Bower wrote no more mining fiction—the surest sign that she had given up hope for a bonanza. New subject matter had since arisen to occupy her interest: In August 1924 a series of articles began appearing in the *San Francisco Examiner* by amateur archeologist Alan Le Baron touting his theory that Nevada was the "cradle" of human civilization. Since debunked, the theory claimed that rock art in the Nevada desert was created not by the ancestors of the local Indigenous people but by a far more ancient Aryan people more closely related to ancient Egypt and Mesopotamia than the local tribes. To make his case, Le Baron claimed that the Nevada rock art contained symbols identical to those found in ancient Egyptian and Babylonian scripts.[92] Le Baron was among a number of archeologists active in the 1920s and '30s—a period of rising white supremacist pseudoscience in America and Europe—attempting to demonstrate the North American origins of human civilization. He convinced the *San Francisco Examiner* editor Edward Clarke to sponsor an expedition to a rock art site thirty miles south of Yerington, which is now the East Walker River Petroglyph Site. The expedition began in May 1924, and a series of articles covering it was published in the *San Francisco Examiner* beginning in August.[93] "Suppose there were white men in California and Nevada 1,000,000 years ago—or even 750,000 years ago! Suppose by the records they left in their wake, they can be traced from that far distant time, through age long migrations across vanished continents, to the spots in Asia and Egypt and Europe where the myths, traditions, legends and histories that constitute our present knowledge of humanity begin!"[94] Le Baron's "discovery" was exactly what Governor Scrugham's board of historical research was looking for to boost Nevada tourism. Appointed to the board in September, Bower was hired by Edward Clarke of the *San Francisco Examiner* to cover Le Baron's explorations in the Black Canyon area in late 1924 and early 1925. Bower set aside the revisions for *Meadowlark Basin*—for which Little, Brown had already paid cash up front—in order to take on this new project.[95]

As part of her research for this work, Bower spent time on location with Le Baron, observing him at work, discussing his findings, and taking photographs of him as he climbed among the rock faces, inspecting his so-called discoveries. On one occasion Dele posed as a sacrificial victim on an outcrop that Le Baron believed functioned as an ancient altar.[96] Bower's role as a writer on the Le Baron expedition was more propagandistic than journalistic. In his correspondence with her about alleged evidence of a human settlement, Le Baron addressed Bower like an employee, dictating the content of a "report" she was to submit to the *San Francisco Examiner* and even treating her as an assistant of sorts: "Would be a good idea for you to come down for *this is a big find.* When you come down, if it is possible to obtain a skull from some doctor please bring it down for a comparison."[97] The fruit of this work was a series of articles about such tantalizing and sensational discoveries as an ancient site of human sacrifice and the remains of an ancient human ancestor—the reason behind Le Baron's request that Bower bring a human skull to the camp.

Bower's archeological writing participated in the larger project of boosting Nevada tourism by appropriating the rock art from the Indigenous people whose ancestors had created them. As western motor tourism expanded, Governor Scrugham looked for ways to attract that traffic to the inhospitable deserts of Nevada. The petroglyphs were a strong candidate for this purpose, especially if their origins could be proven to reside somewhere other than with the displaced Indigenous peoples of Nevada, since it was contradictory to oppress Nevada's Indigenous people while celebrating their cultural achievements. Claiming the petroglyphs as part of their own cultural heritage, Nevada state boosters—Bower among them—touted the theory that the petroglyphs must be the product of ancient Aryan ancestors.

Although Bower's role behind the scenes was to act as Le Baron's promotional arm, in articles like "The Place of Sacrifice" she presents herself as an outside observer and informed citizen. Her own bitter experience in Nevada inflects her portrayal of the state's eccentric history and culture: "Born as a State during the struggle between the North and South, for the sake of the two extra votes it would give to Abraham Lincoln in the Senate; suckled at the favored breast of Dame Fortune during those hectic days of the gold rush, accustomed to having 'men for breakfast' while the Comstock boom was at its height, and taking as a matter of course the daily discovery of bonanza mines—

with such a history, Nevada is not easily excited."[98] Her first order of business upon visiting the site, she tells her readers, is to make sure it is protected from marauding tourists:

> Knowing Nevada so well, I drove home from the ancient Place of Sacrifice in the hills west of Las Vegas, wondering whether the sober citizens would realize the tremendous importance of the discovery; whether the fact that it had stood here under our very noses all this while would not turn those noses up a bit. A chill, drizzly twilight is not the most favorable time for firing the civic enthusiasm of any town, but too often have I seen how quickly and completely a place of interest can be defaced by thoughtless sight-seers, and the Place of Sacrifice is too accessible to escape mutilation unless it is well protected, so when we arrived cold and hungry from our first trip to the new find, I walked straight to the telephone.[99]

Bower doesn't say who she calls, but she implies that her phone call results in efforts by the governor and the Las Vegas Chamber of Commerce to protect the site from "the Johns and the Marys of our land [who] feel that they must leave their own names scratched alongside the Maya snake chronology of archaic men."[100]

From January through March 1925, Bower focused exclusively on her archeological writing, publishing monthly articles in the *San Francisco Examiner*. The work was stimulating but paid poorly, leaving Bower scrambling for the rest of the year to catch up on lost income. That year she completed a novel for *The Popular Magazine* called *The Adam Chasers*, based on her work with Le Baron; revised *Van Patten*, an old unpublished story, for publication in two parts in *Short Stories* and as a novel for Little, Brown; and wrote *White Wolves*, a sequel to her new Montana series that began with *Meadowlark Basin*. The latter was submitted in November—along with a desperate-sounding plea for cash up front—in a rush that coincided with Bower's abrupt move from Las Vegas to Sierra Madre, California. All of this was likely precipitated by more money troubles created by "that confounded mine."[101]

McIntyre rejected *White Wolves* outright, critical of its short length and underdeveloped plot. He advanced Bower $1,500, stipulating that the money was not for *White Wolves* but for a new novel that must "contain a more complicated plot and in every respect measure up to your full length novels."[102] Pretending the rejection had not actually happened, Bower offered to revise the manuscript: "I am quite willing to revise the story as you desire, and to further safeguard you on the investment you have made in it I shall do the work at once."[103] McIntyre capitulated to Bower's version of events: "I . . . am glad to know that you are going to revise 'White Wolves' at once, and I hope you will succeed in giving the story considerably more plot."[104]

Bower's response to this setback and other tactical shifts in her dealings with Little, Brown reveal a change in her relationship with the publisher. She was less trusting and obedient and more willing to take matters into her own hands. For example she no longer left her two main publishers, Little, Brown and *The Popular*, to coordinate the book and serial publication of her work. Little, Brown stuck to their policy of opposing the publication of Bower novels in single-issue magazines, believing this to harm book sales. Little, Brown's policy made it more difficult for Bower to sell her novels to magazines, while *The Popular* continued to ignore it, insisting that the book and magazine markets were entirely separate.[105] Bower had enough of managing spats between Little, Brown and *The Popular*, and she began handling serial publication herself, quietly. When she informed Little, Brown in December of future plans to write fiction about western archeology, she made no mention of the fact that *The Adam Chasers* had already appeared in *The Popular* in May. Nor did she advise them, upon submitting *White Wolves* in November, that a magazine version titled *The White Wolf Pack* had been sent to *The Popular* in September. Having paid the price for previous spats between her two publishers, Bower had evidently decided to control serial publication directly rather than rely on others to abide by their agreements.

Bower's time in Nevada was in some respects a productive and rich experience, but it was fraught with financial anxiety. She poured virtually every cent she earned into El Picacho Mine and saw no returns beyond story ideas. These were quickly transformed into the cash needed to keep the mine running and support Bud, Roy, and Dele. "She thought it would work out like one of her books," her nephew Elmer Muzzy would later reflect.[106] In the end, according to an annotation on a family photo of El Picacho camp, "the mine produced only memories."[107]

5
Days of Little Things

Between the failure of the mine and increasing friction with her publisher, Bower returned to California in a jaded state of mind. Tired of writing "range novels" and inspired by her archeological work, she hinted to Little, Brown that she might quit writing novels altogether. "This may be my last novel for awhile," she wrote in October 1926 about her latest western *Points West*, "since I am once more planning to get away from this particular line of work."[1] Little, Brown had been enthusiastic about her archeological novel *The Adam Chasers*.[2] However, Bower was starting to feel boxed in: "I have several times planned other work, but I find myself always coming back to range novels; I am beginning to wonder if that is my sole mission in life."[3]

She took on no more grand projects, turning her attention to the more conventional and manageable task of buying and improving a house in the suburbs. She and Bud bought two adjacent properties in Sierra Madre, where Bower settled down to write, receive visitors, look after her garden, and enjoy movies and restaurants. She recorded her daily accomplishments, pleasures, and irritations in her diary, which, although destroyed after her death, survives in fragments from the years 1927 to 1929. These fragments are from two different typed copies, one prepared by Dele and the other one probably by Bower. To complicate matters, Bower kept two different versions: a journal that she kept daily—which has been lost—and a revised version that she prepared after the fact as a kind of retrospective exercise. Family members believe that a frustrated Dele destroyed the diary and copies after Little, Brown rejected her biography of Bower.[4] A few pages from the copies survived, providing a rare glimpse into Bower's daily life as a writer . . . before the crash of 1929 changed everything.

Written for an audience of one, diaries can be cryptic and resistant to interpretation. Bower inherited a practical tradition of diary-keeping from her settler ancestors, who needed to keep track of weather patterns, dates of first planting and harvest, crop yields, and major life events like births and deaths. These details were often written quickly in spare moments, with little elaboration or embellishment. Bower's diary is similarly practical and sometimes opaque. Not surprisingly, her livelihood figures prominently; the beginning and completion of stories, as well as the time spent writing them, is meticulously accounted for. The comings and goings of family and friends rank a close second; the identities of many, with abbreviated names like "Mrs. S." or "Mike" have been lost to time. Bower's emotional life is not as well-documented, but she occasionally encoded feelings like happiness, boredom—for which "blah" was her word of choice—depression, or "feeling rather punk," and disappointment. In a confusing twist, two versions of Bower's diary survive from June through September 1927, and there are discrepancies between them. As Bower reviewed and compiled her initial entries into a retrospective, typed revision, she omitted some entries and changed others, sometimes quite significantly. Dele also made changes as she typed Bower's diary, adding commentary or explaining details, occasionally omitting entries that she believed were too private.

Despite these challenges to interpretation, the diaries offer a rare glimpse of Bower's daily life at a time when—once she was no longer sinking every penny into the mine—she could settle into a routine of writing, homemaking, socializing, and generally enjoying her prosperity. Her two adjacent properties on East Laurel Avenue provided plenty of room for Bower, Bud, Dele, Roy—Kitty and Roy had parted, and Roy Jr. stayed with Kitty—and a steady stream of guests. She set about improving the landscaping, planting flowers and climbing vines while Bud and Roy cleared land for an orchard and built a rockery around the outdoor pool. Bower took full advantage of her proximity to Los Angeles, making frequent trips to shop, dine, and attend films and the odd dance performance. In 1927 she saw *Don Juan*, *Old Ironsides*, *Let It Rain*, *Tell It to the Marines*, *The King of Kings*, and *7th Heaven*. She especially loved Cecil B. DeMille's Christian epic *The King of Kings* and went to see it a second time with Dele and a friend in tow. Hardly a week went by when Bower did not either visit or entertain friends, but she also enjoyed quiet time at home spent resting, gardening, housekeeping, or sewing; she made herself two dresses in 1927—one green and one lavender, her favorite color. Her diary frequently makes note of these quiet days with fondness, describing one "day of little things" as "a 'binder' of life, not much in itself but making a composite whole."[5]

Professionally 1927 was less frenzied than Bower's Nevada period had been, and far more lucrative. The 1920s saw an explosion in demand for the genre that Bower herself had been instrumental in popularizing. Street & Smith had launched the first all-western pulp magazine *Western Story* in 1919, which would be followed by dozens of similar publications. With titles like *Masked Rider Western* and *Ranch Romances*, each magazine tried to carve its own distinct niche in the lucrative western fiction market.[6] Once she resigned herself—for now, at least—to writing the range novels that her publishers preferred, Bower received the highest payments of her career for the two novels she completed in 1927: *The Swallowfork Bulls* and a Happy Family novel titled *Hay-Wire*. *The Swallowfork Bulls* was particularly well-received, earning $4,000 for serialization in *Short Stories* and $3,000 from Little, Brown for the book rights—together the equivalent of about $95,000 in present-day values.[7] In *Short Stories*, edited by Harry Maule, a well-known editor and friend of Sinclair Lewis, Bower had finally found a viable alternative to *The Popular* as a venue for her fiction. Maule had begun competing with Charles MacLean for authors, including Bertrand Sinclair, who had serialized his novel *Wild West* in *Short Stories* in 1926.[8] Maule paid well and did not annoy Little, Brown by publishing entire Bower novels in one issue.

On the issue of publicity, Bower had reached a détente with her publishers. She no longer pressed Little, Brown to publicize her identity in their marketing material, but she also made no effort to conceal her identity locally. She made appearances before community groups, bookfairs, and on the radio.[9] But when Little, Brown sent her a questionnaire to be used for publicity, Bower, who just a few years earlier enjoyed the attention she received for her mining work, offered a nondescript response:

> The unusual experiences which were asked for I omitted, perhaps because I have had so many it was difficult to choose any outstanding one. Hobbies I am not aware of, and I believe I have no peculiarities, unless I would be rated peculiar for seeking wisdom rather than pleasure, and in holding the treasures of the mental and spiritual world far above material things. I confess that this does sound peculiar, coming from a writer of Western stories; but I can think of no other eccentricity. If I may say it, my friends and my family seem to find me very livable and human for an author.[10]

Despite recovering financially over the course of 1927, Bower struggled with severe bouts of depression—at least, that is what is suggested by diary fragments and other documents in the archive. She had a history of illnesses described variously in letters to her publisher as "heart and nerve collapse" and "exhaustion," terms often used at the time for what we now call depression and anxiety.[11] Dele's typescript of Bower's diary for the first half of 1927 is peppered with the notation "delete," indicating entries Dele chose not to transcribe, inviting speculation about whether she omitted references to stigmatized mental health conditions. If she did remove references to Bower's depression from her typescript, she did not omit them all; the entry for March 21, 1927, recounts "a day of tired nerves and some depression which I handled as best I could." The next day, after a visit with Dele, who was in her first year at Pomona College, Bower wrote, "Have myself better in hand."[12]

Bower's depression did not prevent her from enjoying her success. She continued to spend her money as quickly as she earned it—not on any grand schemes this time, but on necessities like college for Dele and luxuries like a new Buick and vacation travel. She spent as generously on others as she did on herself, bringing friends and family along on trips to the cinema and vacations, buying clothes for Dele, and never turning away a surprise visitor looking for a place to stay. She kept up the practice of selling her book rights to Little, Brown for quick cash, which cost her untold royalties. According to Bower's records, *Chip of the Flying U* alone sold 1.5 million copies in her lifetime, the proceeds of which Bower saw only a small fraction. Her diary records anxious days waiting for payments and celebratory spending sprees when the checks arrive. When, in April 1927, she received word of Harry Maule's offer of $4,000 for *Swallowfork Bulls*, she bought Dele a new coat, "a beautiful soft warm brown cloth coat with a wide inner lining of fur-fabric in a leopard pattern—very chic," Dele remembered. "I was the envy of the whole dormitory."[13] Two days later a check from Little, Brown came and was immediately spent on a new Buick.

Since acquiring her first automobile in 1911, Bower had become a seasoned driver with a passion for long road trips. This was before the development of the national highway system; most roads were still unpaved and without amenities, making driving a riskier venture than traveling by train or ship. These risks did not deter Bower, as she was already the survivor of at least two car accidents. She routinely drove family and friends for visits and errands and loved the occasional spontaneous excursion. On these jaunts she frequently offered rides to people in need—until she was robbed by a pair of youths in 1928, after which she vowed "never again."[14] Her excitement over the new Buick lasted for the next several days as she took every opportunity to put it through its paces. "A happy day with the new Buick," she wrote after her trip to see *Let It Rain*. "We're still enjoying the new car," she noted two days later. The following Easter Sunday she took Bud and Ruby, Roy's second wife, "to lunch in Hollywood—afterwards to see 'Old Ironsides' after that, a drive through Hollywood and dinner at Marigold Gardens. A perfect day for all."[15]

It was upon returning home from this outing that Bower found her son Harry waiting for her at the Sierra Madre house, along with his wife at the time, Dorothy.[16] Whatever Bower's hesitations had been when Harry had contacted her back in 1924 evaporated at the sight of him on her doorstep: "He and Dorothy from now on will be part of the family. They'll be no burden," she confided to her diary.[17] A few days later, on April 23, Bower took Harry and Dorothy on a sixty-four-mile drive to see her sister Vine, who had recently moved to California after the death of her husband in 1925.[18] She had not seen Harry in more than twenty years. In her diary Bower described the family reunion as "fine" and "harmonious." Having reunited with her estranged son, Bower hatched a plan to reunite Dele with her father, Bill Sinclair. She hadn't seen Bill since their divorce in 1911 when Dele was only five years old, and he now lived in Pender Harbour, British Columbia. "Am very happy over it," wrote Bower in her diary.[19]

With a new novel to write, Bower took the Buick on one more jaunt to Portland, Oregon, with a spontaneous side trip to see Chip in Tacoma, Washington. "A perfect ten days trip," she jotted down in her diary.[20] She then settled down to work on *Hay-Wire*, as well as an eight-thousand-word story commissioned for *The Popular*. She continued to spend time with Dele, entertain friends, go for evening drives, and work on home improvements. As the summer progressed, more visitors showed up at Bower's door. Roy's first wife, now nicknamed Kit, dropped by in June 1927. Then a nephew stayed for three days in mid-June. Early July brought Dele home for the summer. At least one of these visitors brought family drama along with them. Kit, who had been living in Riverside, California, came to visit Bower and Bud on June 25 and decided to stay. Roy Jr.'s whereabouts at this time are unclear; the diary does not mention him. Meanwhile Roy had gone with Ruby to Terre Haute, Indiana, probably in connection with Roy's interest in aviation. Terre Haute was the home of some of the earliest aircraft manufacturers and would have its own airstrip by 1930.[21] Regardless of any awkwardness around Kit's return to the household, Bower welcomed her, writing, "Glad to have Kit here—She is a help."[22] Abruptly, though, Kit changed her plans and left for her home state of Idaho around July 17. While Dele's typescript of the diary reports Kit's return and abrupt departure, Bower left it out when she revised her diary, suggesting that something painful transpired that she preferred not to revisit. Maybe Kit was hoping to reunite with Roy and left when that possibility evaporated.

As soon as *Hay-Wire* was finished, Bower began preparing for the big trip north. She and Dele were to travel by sea to Pender Harbour before Bower continued by train to meet Bud in Chicago. Bower and Bud had both been invited to attend the Chicago rodeo as celebrity guests—Bower for her writing, of course, and Bud for his achievements as a rodeo competitor. Bower spent the month of July shopping for travel clothes, booking tickets, fixing her travel trunk and losing a day's writing when she pounded her finger doing so, all in between writing a last-minute Happy Family story for *The Popular* and looking after the usual steady stream of guests, expected and not. Among these was Paul Eldredge, the ardent Bower fan she befriended in Nevada. The latter arrived unexpectedly and stayed for four days, during which it was decided that he would join Bower and Dele as far as San Francisco. Another wrench was thrown into the works when, less than a week before their scheduled departure, Harry Maule wired to say he could not use *Hay-Wire*, leaving Bower short of money for travel expenses.

With $275 hastily borrowed from the bank, Bower, along with Dele and Paul, boarded the *Emma Alexander* on the morning of July 31, departing San Diego, California, for Victoria, British Columbia, at 11:00 a.m. One of three sister ships belonging to the Admiral Cruise Line, the *Emma* was a 442-foot-long passenger steamship. As Admiral passengers, Bower and her entourage would have been pampered throughout their journey by the mostly African American service staff. African American journalist Thomas Fleming, who worked for Admiral Cruise Lines as a porter in 1926, recalled, "The passenger ships were just like huge floating hotels, and the passengers were pampered. The black crew members were very attentive to taking care of every wish of their guests. We were something like butlers or maids."[23] The entourage enjoyed a "delightful calm afternoon" and an evening of dancing for Paul and Dele. The next day, while the *Emma* was stopped in San Francisco for two nights, the three took a Gray Line bus tour of San Francisco, with stops at Twin Peaks, Golden Gate Park, and the Cliff House, before Paul took his leave. In the evening Bower and Dele took another bus tour of Chinatown. In her diary Bower was lukewarm about the tours: "Mostly blah," she wrote. "We didn't get beyond the surface."[24] She viewed the day more positively, though, when revising her diary after the fact: "Just skimmed the surface of course. . . . But it was all fine and we enjoyed every minute."[25] On their second day in San Francisco, they visited the recently opened M. H. de Young Memorial Museum in Golden Gate Park, where Bower admired John Raphael Smith's print *The Widow of an Indian Chief* and William Wetmore Story's life-size marble *Saul*. The *Emma* sailed for Victoria that afternoon at 5:00 p.m., after which guests were entertained by a masquerade wedding. Bower put makeup on the bridal party, a traveling salesman performed the ceremony, and Dele played the bride.

If Dele was anticipating an emotional reunion with her father upon arrival, that expectation was dashed by a series of mishaps that began when they reached Victoria on the evening of August 4, finding no one waiting to greet them. Unable to find a room at the lavish Empress Hotel, Bower and Dele stayed at a cheap rooming house with a "hard bed" and "no bath."[26] The next day Bill somehow tracked them down, calling the rooming house to let Bower know that he, his wife Ruth, and their daughter Cherry would meet them at the Empress Hotel restaurant. Whatever anxiety Bower felt as she anticipated the reunion was not recorded in her original diary, which relates only typical tourist activities like dining, visiting tourist sites—The Bouchart Gardens and Stanley Park—and shopping with Bower's second cousin Ruth, the woman with whom Bill had broken Bower's heart in 1911. After two days in Victoria and Vancouver, the Bower-Sinclair party left for Pender Harbour early on August 7 aboard Bill's thirty-seven-foot fishing trawler called the Hoo Hoo, a "black-hulled craft that was readily recognized up and down the coast because her stabilizing sail was decorated with a picture of an owl."[27] Oblivious to the fraught history that connected them, Dele and Cherry sang songs while Bower marveled at the exquisite scenery. "A beautiful place this is," she wrote of the intricate system of inlets and coves now hailed on tourist sites as the "Venice of the North."[28] Pender Harbour is part of the traditional territory of the shíshálh Nation, whose ancestors numbered in the thousands before contact but, by the late nineteenth century, had been reduced to a few hundred by smallpox and the intensification of British settlement.[29] When Bower traveled to the land of the shíshálh, she marveled at its many "beautiful but lonely spot[s]" and lagoons "like glass" that were now available for settler tourists to enjoy.[30]

Bower spent three days at "The Stopping Place": Bill's name for his log house overlooking the harbor. To the original structure he had appended rough additions for bedrooms, a new kitchen, a dining room, and a veranda.[31] It was "a dream of a place—a sheltered lagoon" that reminded Bower of the Pocket ranch in Quincy.[32] The presence of other guests meant there were no bedrooms to spare, so Bower and Dele slept in a tent. They spent the next three days observing the abundant wildlife, such as deer and otters, eating fresh-caught fish and oysters prepared by their Chinese cook Charley Chow, watching spectacular sunsets over the Pacific Ocean, swimming in the ocean, exploring the extensive and intricately carved coastline, and listening to the sounds of the tides and the wildlife as they fell asleep at night.

But no amount of natural splendor could overcome the tense relations among Bower, her ex-husband, and his unhappy wife. Ruth and Bill's marriage had been difficult. Ruth resented the financial instability of the writer's life, and she did not share Bill's preference for outdoor living.[33] She had recently returned from an extended stay at the upscale Livermore Sanitarium, where she had been treated for depression at a significant expense, putting further strain on her relationship with Bill—within the year, Ruth would leave Bill for a local oyster farmer.[34] It probably did not help their relationship when Bill took Bower aboard the Hoo Hoo to explore the harbor, showing her how to steer and taking her to his favorite spots. But only a hint of the tension makes its way into Bower's diary—in her entry of August 10: "Folks all milling around. Bill and Ruth not ideal host and hostess. Too selfish." Still the three managed to put on a good show in front of the youngsters. Dele detected no signs of trouble between her parents, and she cheerfully befriended her half sister Cherry. Forty years later Dele would marvel at how oblivious she had been to the tensions that undoubtedly troubled her parents. In a letter to Ivan Ross, her cousin and Bill's nephew, who was also at The Stopping Place that summer, Dele asked,

"Did you know all the undercurrents involved with our elders there? It was amazing—and I know now the whole story—which makes it more amazing—and it is true that truth is stranger than fiction—but only you and I will ever hear the real story—if you care to hear it, for it outpictures all that people do to themselves and others and survive."[35]

After a visit of only a few days, Bower took a boat to Vancouver, British Columbia, on August 12, leaving Dele to spend the rest of the summer in Pender Harbour. From Vancouver, Bower caught a train to St. Paul, Minnesota, en route to the rodeo in Chicago, Illinois. Between meals and games of bridge with her fellow passengers, Bower appreciated the varied landscape outside her window: "Canadian Rockies are magnificent." After the dramatic Rockies came the austere prairie: "Rolling grassland. Desolate ranches." In North Dakota and Minnesota she admired the "fine farms—red barns—white houses." Finally in St. Paul, Bower was met by her sisters Ella and Rose, whom she hadn't seen since her Montana days. "Knew them immediately," she noted. After a two-day visit, Bower headed for Chicago, meeting Bud at the Stevens Hotel. They visited the Art Institute of Chicago in the afternoon before heading to the raucous opening banquet. "[It] was hilarious," she wrote that night. "Shot out the lights n' everything." That incident would get the rodeo party evicted from the hotel, forcing Bower to move to the Blackstone Hotel, where she would room next door to Texas author Owen Payne White.[36]

Promoted as a world championship but in reality attracting competitors mainly from the United States and Canada, the Chicago rodeo was first held in 1925. For the 1927 rodeo, Soldier Field stadium was transformed into a simulated ranch. Hundreds of "bucking horses, calves, longhorn Mexican steers and Brahma steers" were turned loose in the arena while the site was prepared for the event. Celebrity bucking horses were brought from Colorado, Oregon, Wyoming, and elsewhere; with names like Black Powder, Big Bill Thompson, and the never successfully ridden Invalid. Fifty men from the Flathead Reservation, along with their ponies, camped at the stadium while waiting for their turn to compete in segregated races reserved for them.[37] Enticed by the $400,000 purse on offer, as well as the prestige of being a "world champion," competitors from all over North America had been competing in local qualifying events to earn their place at the event.[38]

As invited "guests of the rodeo," Bower and Bud were treated to the preopening banquet and a luncheon on opening day before appearing in the grand opening parade on Saturday afternoon. On Saturday at 3:00 p.m. Bower and Bud joined western writers Will James and Ross Santee—along with hundreds of other guest celebrities, competitors, and performers—outside Soldier Field to await their turn to make the grand entrance. In her 1928 Flying U novel *Rodeo*, Bower described the scene through the eyes of The Kid, son of Chip and the fictional Della, now a grownup rodeo competitor:

> Out in the hazy sunlight the Kid blinked at the spectacle before him on the gentle slope before the white façade of the museum. When last he had seen that slope it had been empty, a wide expanse of lawn with the roadway running down at the side like a binding on a green velvet robe. Two hundred horsemen stood there now in double column, with more galloping alongside, anxious to find their places in the lines. Flag-draped automobiles, Indians in gay beaded costumes and war bonnets of eagle feathers. Two great flags fluttered at the head of the column down by the gate; and beyond them lay the huge coliseum with its steep slopes of massed humans and the distant droning as if all the bees in the world had gathered buzzing there. . . . Suddenly the loud blare of a band, amplified until it seemed to the Kid that they were playing close beside him, swung into the heady rhythm of "The Stars and Stripes Forever." The column began to move forward, the horses taking little nipping steps as if they too felt the exhilaration of that martial music. As they swept down the slope and into the arena waves of applause surged up to meet them.[39]

The rodeo lasted for more than a week, culminating in the finals on Monday, August 29. Bower attended every day, taking in the men and women bronc riders—women would be excluded from rough stock events in 1929—calf roping, steer wrestling, relay races, and trick riding.[40] She took time out from the rodeo to have a dentist grind down a broken tooth, meet with Harry Maule, make a guest appearance on a local radio station, attend various dinners and luncheons, and sample Chicago's infamous club scene. Her diary cryptically alludes to one late night at a club called "Chez Paree"—perhaps the underground forerunner to the more famous club that opened in 1932, just after prohibition ended. When Bower later transcribed her diary she filled in more details, referring to "Chez Pierre" as "a noted Cabaret." She "made off with trophies—an indecent menu card and two Apollinaris jugs," presumably used to serve illicit alcohol. The next day it was "quiet around the rodeo headquarters, everybody feeling the effects of last night." Later that week Bower lunched at a brewery where she drank "real, illegal beer."[41]

The rodeo ended anticlimactically for Bower with a rainy day of finals, which she described as "blah—not all of it though."[42] In the marquee event, a new bronc riding champion, Floyd Stillings, was crowned, and Florence Hughes won the highly competitive cowgirl trick riding competition.[43] The next day Bower drove a borrowed car to Terre Haute, Indiana—a journey of several hours—to visit Roy and Ruby. After a "good visit," Bower drove back to Chicago, arriving very late and getting up in time for the 5:30 a.m. train to Denver, the first leg of her journey home. "THIS HAS BEEN A WONDERFUL MONTH! MY FIRST REAL VACATION IN YEARS," she later reflected in her revised diary.[44] It was to be Bower's last opportunity to appreciate the perks of being an almost-celebrity writer with the time and resources for travel, restaurants, clubs, and parties. Although no one knew it yet, the crash of 1929 and the Great Depression were about to put an end to the frivolities for Bower and many others.

The letdown began with Bower's trip home, which, to borrow Bower's words, was "not so good." The economy lunch of cheese, pickles, and cookies served on the train made her "sick as a dog."[45] After a miserable stopover in Denver, Colorado, Bower and Bud detoured to Laramie, Wyoming, where they spent a few days visiting Bud's childhood home and nearby historic sites such as Sherman's monument and the ruins of Fort Sanders. The great plains landscape triggered painful memories for Bower, who had been a trapped housewife when she last lived there: "Interesting trip but depressing country for me," she wrote.[46] Her view changed, however, in her later transcription, when she remembered the drive to Bud's old home as "a beautiful trip" and a visit to the elderly Mary Powell, whose husband had been murdered by the legendary outlaw Tom Horn, as "a big day."[47] After the detour to Laramie, Bower and Bud returned to Denver to catch their train for home. During the four-day last leg of their journey, Bower's darkened mood is reflected in her relative indifference to the scenery. She was "not so much impressed" by the Royal Gorge in Colorado. When the train passed the Pocket ranch after dark, Bower tried to make out what remained of it but could see very little. On the morning of September 12, Bower and Bud arrived in San Francisco where they took in some shows while waiting for the evening train to Glendale. Capping off the depressing return journey, Bower's train to Glendale hit a man on the tracks.[48] It was an ominous ending to Bower's last vacation.

6

Readjustments

Upon her return to Sierra Madre in mid-September 1927, Bower was immediately confronted by a pile of bills and more disappointing news from the mine, this time in the form of a disillusioning report from an expert identified in her diary as "Captain."[1] Various domestic tasks and writing projects distracted Bower from these worries. As usual she had a house full of family and friends: Roy and Ruby, with Ruby's brother Fred in tow, and Dele, just returned from Pender Harbour and about to go back to college. Bower helped her sew new curtains for her dorm room before seeing her off. That same day she started work on the galley proofs for *Points West*, which had just arrived. She spent the rest of the month working on three different writing projects at various stages, installing a garden pond, and going to shows with Roy, Ruby, and Fred. Roy and Fred helped install the pond and plant it with lilies, cattails, rushes, and irises. They stocked it with goldfish from Goldfish Gardens in Culver City, California. "As perfect as we can make it," she wrote. "Nature must do the rest."[2]

During her stay in Pender Harbour, Bower may have compared notes with Bill about the prices she was getting for her stories, for she was unusually assertive when negotiating with MacLean for serial rights to *Hay-Wire*. After it had been turned down by *Short Stories*, almost ruining her vacation plans in the process, Bower had submitted it to *The Popular*, and MacLean readily accepted it. Bower negotiated hard, perhaps recognizing that MacLean depended on her to fill his magazine more than he cared to admit. Twice in 1927 Bower had received last-minute requests for stories that no longer came to him automatically.

She insisted upon and received $3,500 for serial rights to *Hay-Wire*. "A real achievement," she wrote in her diary.[3] When the check arrived in mid-October, she promptly ordered another new Buick. While her negotiating skills had much improved, her money management had not.

Bower's diary for this period is ominously unaware of what is to come. It records visits to and from friends and family, trips to movies and shows, checks received, tasks completed, and good works accomplished. Full of ideas inspired by her visit to Chicago, Bower began her new novel *Rodeo* in early November and worked on it steadily in between celebrating a string of holidays with family. "[Fifty-six] good hard years of living and still going strong," she wrote on November 15, 1927—her birthday. One week later she spent a busy Thanksgiving cooking for eight, making "a very pretty table," and washing dishes while the "kids did acrobatic stunts." On December 24 she and Bud drove to Long Beach, California, to spend Christmas with Roy and Ruby. Bower noted, "A nice, happy evening, though it rained most of the time."[4]

On the way home from Long Beach, Bower and Bud witnessed an accident scene, the description of which is a jarring departure from the normality of family life and daily work. In a diary that is more workmanlike than confessional, Bower's response to the experience stands out for what it reveals about her worldview: "Hudson Sedan ran into a freight train. The driver and his wife killed—a child about 2 years probably killed. The mother and two little girls cut and bruised. Did what we could—too little, though. . . . My first contact with violent death." Shaken by the experience, Bower and Bud narrowly escaped an accident of their own: "Destruction walked abroad. Bud nearly ran over a man and almost collided with another car."[5] An unwavering automobile enthusiast no matter how many accidents she experienced, Bower saw these mishaps as the mystical result of contagious bad luck.

She soon recovered from the experience, completing fourteen chapters of *Rodeo* by the end of the year and needing rubber caps to protect her fingers as she typed. "A marvelous year," she wrote on the eve of 1928.[6] All indications were that life in 1928 would continue as before, with Bower scrambling to write enough to pay her bills, distracted from that task by a busy family and social life. Dele made frequent trips to and from college, and she had also enlisted Bower to type a college paper for her. Harry wrote with news that he was coming to Los Angeles, his marriage to Dorothy having crumbled. If the purchase of a second car was meant to ease some of this pressure on Bower by giving Dele and Bud more independence, the plan backfired, creating a "domestic storm," Bower noted in her diary, when the two clashed over the Buick.[7] Small details like this reveal much about Bower's role in the household: busy with deadlines and responsibilities, she would sometimes spend lavishly to keep the peace.

Although Bower was under pressure to complete *Rodeo* so that she could request a check from Little, Brown, her diary notes without complaint the many interruptions by friends and family. "We are rather crowded but are happy," she wrote of one particularly busy weekend when some seven guests milled about. A generous friend, Bower would often drop what she was doing to go for a drive, bring a friend home for dinner, or even bail them out of jail.[8] Among her closest friends were her cousin Lydia, writer Marah Ellis Ryan—known affectionately as "sister Ryan" in Bower's diary—and a woman known mysteriously as "Mike" (quotation marks in original). Bower's contacts in the film industry included Hollywood agents Les and Dorothy Feader, who represented Bower for the film industry and were also good friends and fellow Christian Science adherents. Bower was a trusted confidante. Parting after a long visit, the mysterious "Mike" told her that their talk "did her good."[9] Bower organized a picnic to get another friend "out of convent notion"—although who would be going to a convent, and why, is unclear.[10]

Having become wise to the workings of the publishing process and all but exhausting Little, Brown's flexibility with cash advances, Bower was not above the occasional ruse to secure faster payments for a manuscript. When she was unable to finish *Rodeo* before the money ran out, Bower knowingly submitted the manuscript with the last chapter unwritten, hoping the publisher wouldn't notice before the payment was processed.[11] The ploy worked, and a payment was issued before a first reading revealed that the manuscript was incomplete. Bower had already written and posted the missing chapter by the time Little, Brown had sent her a terse letter demanding it "at once." Bower responded to this demand with a cleverly worded explanation: "I discovered Chapter Twenty Two, and have sent it to you."[12]

With yet another financial fire put out, an opportunity arose that tantalized Bower with the prospect of financial stability: she secured an introduction to western film star Hoot Gibson. Born Edmund Richard Gibson, Hoot had transitioned from ranch work to Wild West shows to film and also won titles as a rodeo competitor. He had already starred in film adaptations of several Bower novels, most notably as Chip in the 1926 feature version of *Chip of the Flying U* produced by Universal Pictures. In their meeting on January 26, 1928, Gibson expressed interest in seven more Bower stories—"a full year's program," Bower wrote in her diary. Bower's relief is palpable as her diary pages describe several days of celebratory indulgence; the entire family went on an excursion, stopping for lunch in Victorville, California, before hiking to an abandoned mine in the mountains outside of Los Angeles. Bud and Bower left the youngsters to camp while they stayed at the newly built Melrose Hotel in Hollywood.[13] The next day Bower and Bud rejoined the camp and cooked a rabbit dinner. "Kids having a wonderful time," she wrote of the trip.[14] After the weekend away, Bower treated herself to a day of shopping and a trip to the beauty parlor for a facial.

These celebrations were premature; Hoot failed to contact Bower to close the deal. A week after their meeting, Bower's diary betrays growing anxiety. "I am just waiting," she wrote on February 2. The next day: "Still waiting on the Hoot Gibson deal." After two more days of waiting, Bower took action, consulting an old friend from her early days in the film business: "This pm I suddenly called Selig and went to see him. Got information." Now at the end of his career, Selig had filmed Bower's early novels, including *Chip of the Flying U*, and could offer her insider knowledge and advice. The next day Bower contacted Universal Pictures and arranged a meeting with Hoot. It was "a perfect conference lasting until 3 pm," during which Hoot and Bower discussed the stories he would use for his films. Bower was also to play a more significant role in the adaptation process, which she hoped would save her stories from the sensationalism and melodrama that afflicted other film westerns. After the meeting Bower made sure her agent, Les Feader, followed up with Hoot while she saw to other obligations, including parents' day at Dele's college. When the good news finally came, Bower wrote that she was "tired but happy." She explained, "I went to see Dele and take her some flowers. In the evening Les called he has closed the deal with Hoot Gibson." All the signs were now pointing to a fruitful year of adapting seven Bower stories to film for Hoot. Bower made several trips to Hollywood for meetings with the general manager, continuity man, and publicist. She saw Hoot Gibson's latest films *Flying Fists* and *Painted Ponies* and attended film shoots to see him work. She hired a secretary and began work on a home office, something she hadn't had since her writing cabin at the mine.[15]

With relief from financial pressure came other preoccupations. Like many women influenced by the recently popularized concept of calorie counting and the idealization of the boyish flapper body, Bower started a weight-loss and fitness regimen.[16] She went on an orange and grapefruit diet and signed up for dance classes at Norma Gould's studio. Gould was a pioneer of modern dance and ran a popular studio where she taught "all phases of dance."[17] Her eponymous dance troupe made frequent appearances at community events throughout Los Angeles. Bower purchased a dance costume complete with dance slippers, and she began attending dance class two to three times per week, reporting in her diary that it helped her manage her fatigue. "Not so tired either, tonight. The dancing helps!"[18]

Influenced by the Feaders, Bower continued her practice in Christian Science. After visiting Sawtelle veterans' hospital with her Christian Science study class, she began regular visits to the hospital with gifts of oranges, magazines, and nosegays to "pin on the boys." Christian Science taught (and still does) that Bower could achieve healing in all aspects of life—"health, relationships, finances, or environment," according to its website—through living according to the spiritual laws of God that can be learned, understood, and proven through healing and regeneration.[19] In her diary Bower recorded the progress of her spiritual practice and signs of "harmony" in her life.

Hopeful developments at the mine may well have affirmed Bower's faith. Bud still hadn't given up on what had been his brainchild. He continued to work the mine on a regular basis, often with the help of Roy or some other relative. In her novel *The Parowan Bonanza*, Bower's protagonist Hopeful Bill persists, much like Bud did, despite the collapse of his mining corporation. Having learned his lesson, Hopeful Bill continues to work the mine on a smaller scale, with only the help of his wife and daughter. Bower rewards this family-centered—and unrealistic—approach to mining with a modest but sustainable lode that promises to support the family for the years to come. Perhaps she had her own family in mind when she crafted this ending, for Bower's mine had become a family affair: Roy, Ruby, Ruby's brother Fred, and Dele's boyfriend Dick all went to the mine in early February 1928 while Bower was still waiting to hear about the Hoot Gibson deal. A day after she celebrated closing the deal by making dinner for Les and Dorothy Feader, she received a letter from Roy along with a sample that was promising enough for Bower to visit the mine herself. In late February she took time out from her meetings and office preparations to "see how work was going."[20] Once she arrived Roy showed her samples of "high grade silver." The next day she and Roy took more samples and "ran into what seems to be a sample of *horn silver*. Can hardly believe it." Upon returning from the mine, Bower was still in a state of disbelief: "Still trying to realize our good fortune in the rich strike. Bud a bit flighty but will calm down."[21] Bower linked her good fortune to her faith: "February has been a good month," she wrote in her diary, "and my area is cleared for much action in future. I give thanks for increased fruitfulness in all channels."[22] Although the test results from the mine assays would not be available for two weeks, her confidence in the strike was such that she purchased a lot at a new development adjacent to the Belmont Country Club, located near what is now Verdugo Mountain Park, offering easy access to golf, horseback riding, hiking, and scenic surroundings.[23]

Professionally Bower's preoccupation was now with her film work. She met with the continuity man at Universal Pictures to discuss the filming of her novel *Points West*, made preparations to attend one of

Hoot's film shoots in Bishop, Nevada, and started on a film "treatment" of her newest novel *Hay-Wire*. Needing a dedicated workspace to meet the coming demand for scenarios and titles, she enlisted Harry's help painting and wallpapering her new office. But with no deadlines immediately looming and money in the bank, Bower also took advantage of the opportunity to enjoy all of the pleasures that spring in Southern California had to offer, fitting in her love of films and theater every chance she could. A shopping trip, meeting, or errand usually meant dinner and a show with whoever happened to be around. She treated Harry to the musical comedy *Hit the Deck* and, along with Dele and "Mike," the war film *Wings*, which would go on to be the first Academy Award Winner for Best Picture. She had lunch with friends at the Wistaria Fete, an annual event celebrating the blooms of the famous wistaria vine of Sierra Madre, first planted in 1884 and still alive today.[24] She hosted a dinner party with film business friends and paid visits to her sister Vine and cousin Lydia, among other friends and family. And of course she did not neglect her garden, enlisting Roy and Harry to plant dahlia bulbs and a rose arbor. Her new goldfish were an ongoing concern, and she noted when they met mishaps: "Roy stepped on the smallest fish, so now I have six."[25] When one of them, named Charley, disappeared, she drained the pond to find him.[26] She made a special trip to Goldfish Gardens in Culver City to confirm that she had baby fish in her pond and not tadpoles.[27]

It's hard to identify the turning point, the moment, day, or event that marked the end of rising prosperity and the beginning of a steady decline. The Stock Market Crash of 1929 has been mythologized as a short, sharp division between the optimism and excess of the twenties and the bleak austerity of the thirties, but the transition was experienced in various ways. For the people of the Santa Clara River Valley, the collapse of the St. Francis Dam shortly before midnight on March 13, 1928, flooding the valley and killing more than 450 people, marked an end to the carefree living of the 1920s.[28] For Bower, the turning point may have begun the following day. As news of the disaster monopolized the front page of the *Los Angeles Times*, she took her adult children to the Belmont Country Club to show them the new lot. On the way home they stopped in Los Angeles to get the results of the assays from the strike at El Picacho Mine. "Not so good," Bower wrote in her diary that day. "Same old incline ore."[29] It was the first of several setbacks that would continue to pile up for the next year. Three days after the flood, Bower did something strange: "went to morgue and saw eight victims of flood at Santa Paula."[30] Her diary does not explain her motives for doing so, but the entry describing the car accident she had seen in late 1927 suggests that Bower regarded such events as portentous. Her diary entry for the end of March summarized the month as one of "growing consciousness of the actions of the One Mind, the One Life."[31] That her disappointment came upon the heels of a disaster so close to home may have been one of those "actions."

Still, in that same diary entry, Bower congratulated herself for not experiencing a "setback" or depressive episode, and, with her new office complete, focused on the Hoot Gibson deal. She completed two adaptations of Flying U stories for film by the end of April: *Hay-Wire* and *Meadowlark Basin*. Having not received a check since early March and with property and income tax bills due, money became tight, but Bower tried to remain optimistic. "April has seen some changes," she wrote in her diary, "but a growth as well as slight readjustment. The money angle remains a problem, but I'll solve it, I *know*" (Bower's emphasis).[32] May began with a return of "the doldrums," followed by several days of blank pages in Bower's diary, which likely indicated a bout of depression. Whatever the reason, she regained her productivity, starting a new novel titled *Fool's Goal* while she waited to hear from Hoot Gibson about the screenplays she had already written. Otherwise life on the whole was low-key in comparison to the spring. Trips to shows and restaurants tapered off—although Bower did not completely give up the movies she loved so dearly. When Dele needed new clothes in preparation for a second summer with Bill in Pender Harbour, they were homemade rather than store-bought. Bower's social life consisted of entertaining "sister" Ryan or the Feaders at home. Her volunteer work at the hospital continued; she would spend entire days making boutonnieres for "the boys" at Sawtelle, pinning on as many as 190 the next day.[33]

Although Bower had completed two film treatments for Hoot Gibson, she had heard nothing from him since they had met in late February. Finally in mid-June 1928, Bower learned that Hoot had agreed to film *Rodeo* on location at the Chicago rodeo. Bower herself had persuaded her contacts at the rodeo to advance $2,500 for Hoot's trip to Chicago, which likely helped Hoot make up his mind. There are signs, however, that Bower was starting to resent the treatment she was receiving: when Hoot enlisted her to ghostwrite an article for him, she wrote rather tersely of the experience in her diary, "I wrote it, (he signs it). . . . Feel rather punk."[34] The good news about *Rodeo* came with a blow: Bower learned from Les Feader that *Rodeo* was the only Bower story Hoot would be making. Whatever deal had been made in February for "a full year's program" of Bower stories was not one that worked in Bower's favor. Bower was to be paid $1,000 for rights to *Rodeo*, supervising the production, and writing titles.[35] Or, at least, that is what she thought. Bower soon learned that she would not be traveling with Hoot to film in Chicago nor was her input welcomed for the parts of the film shot in Los Angeles, as this diary entry reveals: "Went to Universal to see Hoot work on *Rodeo*. Saw I was superfluous and left early."[36]

All the same, Bower took these blows in stride. "This June was a harmonious and fruitful month—filled with 'faith and good works,'" she wrote in her diary. From the time her check for *Chip of the Flying U* had financed her first divorce, Bower had always been able to count on her writing to get her through periods of personal and financial setbacks. She had a substantial sum from *Rodeo* and was already working on *Fool's Goal*, which she could expect to see her through the next several months. What she didn't realize when she made her optimistic diary entry for the month of June was that one of her major markets was in the process of collapsing. On June 17, just one day before she had learned the bad news about the Hoot Gibson deal, Charles MacLean, the editor of *The Popular*, who had discovered Bower more than twenty years ago, died. Bower would not learn of his death until almost two weeks later. The event was to mark the end of her twenty-four-year relationship with *The Popular*—and eventually the demise of the magazine itself—cutting Bower's income in half.[37] It was a personal loss as well. Although MacLean had played a significant role in perpetuating Bower's relative anonymity as an author and had sometimes played fast and loose with the serial rights to her stories, he had been a constant presence in her life since she had published her first "hit" story in his magazine. Bower's contribution to a commemorative book about MacLean was probably more sincere than not in its recollection of his importance to her: "Year after year, story after story; pink letters at first (and I have them all), then blue; arguments, felicitations, mutual sympathy." She recalled an exchange of letters, which is one of the few surviving records of their correspondence:

> I shall never forget that spring of ill health and nervous tension when he wrote, 'Aren't you working too hard? These last stories seem to lack some of the punch we expect from you.' I was working under contract then, and the contract 'rode' me day and night. I told him so. He replied with one of those warm, human, understanding letters which only MacLean could write. 'Forget that contract,' said he. 'Write what you please when you please, and don't worry.' And he volunteered a substantial raise in the price. . . . So the friendship grew. I have his understanding and sympathy woven into the pattern of my life as a writer.[38]

It took time for the effects of MacLean's death to confront Bower directly. Indeed she enjoyed a productive but relaxing summer. With money in the bank from her *Rodeo* deal with Universal, Bower's finances still seemed relatively sound. *Rodeo* had earned $6,400 in serial and book rights alone, so Bower could reasonably expect a comparable sum for *Fool's Goal* when it was finished. And with Bud at the mine and Dele at Pender Harbour, she had ample time to work. She spent the month of July writing *Fool's Goal* and working on the production and publicity of *Rodeo*. She took time out for trips to the movies, and she tried her hand at golf at the Belmont Country Club. Lydia and her family arrived for a visit in their new Hudson automobile. Roy was trying his hand at writing, and Bower helped him with the logistics of submissions and as a creative sounding board. The goldfish in the pond continued to multiply.

The film version of *Rodeo* was to be somewhat of a comeback for Bower—an attempt to bring her Flying U stories into the modern world, rekindle the success she had with the early Flying U novels, and open up more opportunities for Bower in the film industry. These intentions are made clear in the film's opening titles: "Who does not cherish a memory of the old West . . . Those good old days at the Flying U Ranch—and 'Chip,' the idol of that 'Happy Family'? . . . today, that memory has become the guiding star for a modern 'Chip'—the image of his father—a new 'Chip of the Flying U.'"[39] The film tells the story of Montana Kid—the grown son of Chip and Della—as he leaves Montana to become a rodeo star in Chicago. The opening titles reminded viewers of their affection for Chip and the Happy Family, promising them another story in the beloved series. Rather than waxing nostalgic for the old West of the late nineteenth century, however, the film embraced the modern West of performance, spectacle, and urban life. Figuring rodeo competition as the means by which cowboys can integrate into the modern world, the film features extensive footage of rodeo events filmed on location at the Chicago rodeo in 1928 as a stadium of spectators looked on. When Chip gets entangled in a robbery and a case of mistaken identity, viewers are also treated to an elaborate car chase through the busy streets of Chicago.

Having resented the sensationalism and lack of realism in past adaptations of her novels, Bower took pains to ensure she would be more involved in the film production of *Rodeo*. She met with screenwriter George Morgan, as well as Hoot, hopeful that her involvement would result in a film both authentic and true to her writing.[40] Although the plot of *Rodeo* had to be whittled down considerably for film, it still bears Bower's stamp, initiating viewers into an unfamiliar world—not of a Montana cattle ranch, but of competitive rodeo—and emphasizing humor and realistic detail. In the opening scene, the Montana Kid, played by Hoot Gibson of course, is practicing for a relay race—a rodeo event in which cowboys ride a "string" of horses in succession, changing tack in between mounts. As the main plot unfolds, viewers are also educated about how cowboys prepare for this event—details Bower probably learned during her trip to the Chicago rodeo the previous year. As the Montana Kid puts his horses through their paces, his cowboy friends, the aptly named Shorty and Slim, look on, the latter with a stopwatch in hand. This was not standard popular western fare, with its emphasis on nostalgia and violence.

Bower took an interest in the publicity campaign for *Rodeo*. She wrote to Little, Brown to advise them about the forthcoming production, which was to follow directly on the heels of the serial version appearing in *The Popular* in the fall. She encouraged Little, Brown to similarly coordinate the book publication with the release of the film. An avid moviegoer herself, Bower recognized the medium's growing cultural importance and potential to invigorate the book industry. Several breakthrough films had recently been released, including the WWI aviation film *Wings*, which impressed audiences with its air-battle sequences and win of the first Oscar for Best Picture, and *The Jazz Singer*, the first feature-length "talkie" that included not only dialogue but recorded music and synchronized singing. When Bower saw the latter in the summer of 1928 she had loved it so much that she went back to see it again.

The male-dominated worlds of book and film production were not always receptive to Bower's forays outside of her role as a fiction writer. Her conservative publisher was skeptical that moving pictures—still relatively lowbrow with a twenty-five-cent admission—could help sell two-dollar books, and they stuck to their plan to publish *Rodeo* in the summer of 1930.[41] Universal Studios was a busy and raucous environment where few women worked in positions of authority. Schedules were extremely tight; entire films were produced and released within the space of a few months, which left little time for consulting over the finer details such as the right kind of saddlery or the correct breed of horse—nuances that Bower cared deeply about. Few attempts were made to make the outskirts of Los Angeles look like Montana for the production of *Rodeo*. The Kid's childhood home is clearly a Los Angeles bungalow, and the southwestern desert, having always sufficed as the go-to western setting of film, would have to do for her home state of Montana as well.

When *The Popular* rejected *Fool's Goal* in early September, Bower didn't panic. She reverted to lessons she had learned in her earliest days as a writer and sent the manuscript to the next publisher on her list: *Blue Book Magazine*, one of the top pulps of the 1920s. When *Blue Book Magazine* also returned the manuscript, she submitted it to *Short Stories,* also a top circulating pulp. While she waited for word from *Short Stories* editor Harry Maule, she worked on other things. The titles for *Rodeo* were due, and they were a daunting task; well-executed titles were considered integral to the quality of a film, and their function was more complex than to simply convey dialogue. In his 1913 article, director Charles Gaskill advised that the title "must indicate the logic, the poetry, the sentiment, the philosophy and other abstract qualities found in the picture—it must illuminate."[42] The completed titles had to be painted or stenciled onto a specially prepared decorative background and then transferred to the film, all in time for the October preview.[43] Bower went to Universal Studios on September 21 to watch the completed footage of *Rodeo*, receiving a traffic ticket after running a stop sign in the process. She then wrote the titles over the next two days, was "very well pleased" with them, and met with the director and film editor at Universal Studios for the finishing touches.

Bower's work on *Rodeo*—which was released as *King of the Rodeo* in January 1929—coincided with a political debate in California in which she took a particular interest. Dubbed the "anti-rodeo bill," Proposition 21 would prohibit "terrifying or exciting" animals "for sport, exhibition, or amusement," effectively putting an end to rodeos in the state.[44] More or less disregarding her publishers' strictures against publicity, Bower became one of the most high-profile and vocal opponents of the bill, leveraging her reputation as a western authority to criticize the bill in newspaper articles and public talks. Rodeos, Bower claimed, did not abuse animals but provided them with outlets for behaviors that came naturally to them: "Bucking, running races with the herd, kicking and snorting and bawling, [horses] behave very much as they do at rodeos under the saddle. Cattle also buck and kick and run just for the sport of it."[45] She and Bud organized a demonstration on the eve of the election to oppose the proposition; 250 riders, including star rodeo competitors and trick riders, formed a cavalcade at Sunset and Vine before marching through the streets of Los Angeles.[46]

Bower's financial straits continued into the fall of 1928. She focused on writing short fiction for quick cash while Harry, Roy, and Ruby looked for work. Harry had been job hunting since the spring, when he was turned down by the navy. He had tried for various manual labor jobs—working on a boat, driving a milk truck, painting an airline hangar—without success. Roy and Ruby took on a job delivering directories, but after only one day they found the job "unprofitable" and quit.[47] All of these measures were taken as stopgaps until Bower was able to sell the serial rights for *Fool's Goal* for her next big infusion of cash. When Harry Maule turned it down for *Short Stories*, family finances reached a crisis point. "Readjustments," Bower wrote in her diary. "Family standing by."[48] These "readjustments" included a scramble to find another publisher for *Fool's Goal*, long days of writing more stories, and a trip to Pomona College to deliver the bad news to Dele that she might have to drop out. According to Bower's diary, Dele was "game to leave school if necessary."[49] Her new beau Alex Baird may have been a factor in her decision; the two were married by the following April.

For all of her money worries, Bower summed up 1928 optimistically in her diary as if trying to convince herself that the setbacks of the fall were temporary: "Professionally I have advanced almost double my old rate, and have a wider market . . . I had a marvelous summer. I am doing much better work. This has been a year of broad service in new channels—the hospital work particularly."[50] She did have moderate successes in early 1929, including the sale of two stories of a new series to *Everybody's Magazine*—a new market for Bower—but these were not enough to stave off mounting bills. Dele did not return to college in the new year. In February Bud was diagnosed with cardiac asthma, and Bower sold her beloved Buick. By the end of March, the goldfish Bower had so fondly tended to were sold, and she and Bud left the Sierra Madre house for an apartment in Los Angeles.

They tried to make a go of it in Los Angeles. Having found a new magazine publisher, *Everybody's Magazine*, for her *Tiger Eye* novel, it seemed as though Bower's serial market was back on track. Her diary records no sense of loss as she adjusted to her new home in the spring of 1929, setting up the new apartment, hosting visitors, going to the movies, and shopping for Dele's wedding dress. "Took my first ride on top of a bus," she reported as if on a tourist excursion. Within days of the move, Dele and Alex were married in the Los Angeles apartment. "A perfect wedding which will live in my memory always," Bower wrote in her diary. Having left Sierra Madre before she had an opportunity to see her new garden mature, she and Bud took a streetcar to their old neighborhood to see "how things were growing."[51]

After the wedding Bower set up a study and tried to fill the hole left when *The Popular*, jittery after the death of its chief editor, cut back on its new acquisitions. In the context of general economic decline, which hindsight teaches us was a precursor to economic devastation, Bower managed to publish two short stories for a few hundred dollars each. Her agent, Paul Reynolds—taken on to help Bower negotiate the shifting magazine fiction market—would eventually sell serial rights to *The Long Loop*, completed in the fall of 1929, for $4,000, which would be Bower's last hurrah in the periodical market.

After the October stock market crash dashed any hopes of a quick recovery, Bower tried to diversify. She jumped at the chance to enter a collaboration with film actors Wallace Coburn and Nils Chrisander to produce an epic film based on the origin stories of the Blackfeet. In great detail Bower wrote to McIntyre about the project and the men behind it. Both were fascinated by—and seeking to profit from—Indigenous culture. Montana-born Coburn ran his own production company and claimed to be an adopted member of the Blackfeet who "[knew] their customs and life better than most white men." Chrisander, a Swede, had been a film star in Europe before traveling the globe to study "the ancient religions of the world as they have seeped into the savage tribes."[52] Claiming to have been "given" the story of Manitou by the Blackfeet, Coburn approached Bower to write the scenario, as well as a novel, based on the film.

Bitter experience had taught Bower to cut her losses sooner rather than later. Within a few months, she backed out of the film project "because of the officiousness and egotism of [Coburn]. It would be almost impossible to do good work with such a personality."[53] She did, however, maintain ties with Chrisander, collaborating with him on a semi-biographical novel based on his life as a European film star, witness to postwar devastation, and pursuit of "esoteric wisdom with a Master of the Himalayas," among other topics.[54] Without consulting Little, Brown about their willingness to publish this departure from her usual fare, Bower submitted a manuscript titled "That Other Country" in April, asking for an advance of $600. The tactic set off another spat with her publisher; Little, Brown obliged her with an advance, but not for the Chrisander novel, which the publisher believed would disappoint Bower's current readers without attracting any new ones.[55] This left Bower owing Little, Brown another novel while fomenting longstanding resentments. "Your letter astonished me," she wrote in reply to McIntyre's rejection. "About once in ten years I have rebelled against my job of being just 'Bower'. . . . And 'Little, Brown' just sits tight until it's over."[56] Without apologizing exactly, she promised to be "safe and sane for another ten years" and requested an advance of $1,000 for what she promised would be a more conventional Bower book.[57] Bower submitted "That Other Country" to another publisher under a pseudonym. There is no record of its publication, and the manuscript has since been lost.

The debacle over "That Other Country" left Bower scrambling. After losing even more valuable writing time on an aborted Texas novel, she wrote Little, Brown again in November 1930, hat in hand, for another advance, placating them with the promise of a story of "the Happy Family as it used to be."[58] She completed this novel, *Dark Horse*, in January 1931, quickly following it up with *Laughing Water* in April. Both novels were written hastily, and it showed. At sixty thousand words, *Dark Horse* was five to ten thousand words shorter than her usual word length. In a scolding letter to Bower, Little, Brown demanded that she lengthen *Laughing Water* by eight thousand words. "Your readers expect more in the way of value in number of words."[59] Bower's readers had also noticed that her latest novels were on the short side. Of *The Long Loop* one British librarian complained, "Big type, heavily spaced, and wide margin, many a story in a 6d [six penny] magazine is longer. . . . One has sometimes to put with an author with a *big reputation* trading on his name in this manner, but this! . . . The first reader who took it from the Library passed the remark that it would be read in half an hour."[60] *Dark Horse* received similar complaints from Bower's British publishers Hodder & Stoughton, who told Little, Brown they would have to sell the book at a lower price because of its reduced length.[61]

Bower's only income now consisted of advances from Little, Brown on novels yet to be written, even as she was required to revise and lengthen those already submitted. "I have sold nothing at all to the magazines for a year and a half," she told Little, Brown in mid-1931:

Such property as I have kept is a liability rather than an asset. . . . With lead and silver lower than they have ever been in my knowledge, the mine has been a flock of white elephants. Furthermore, my husband has been ill for three years now, and I have to carry on alone. . . . So you see, illness as well as business depression force me to borrow sometimes to bridge the gap. I'll try to keep the stream fordable—or at least to find fords so that the bridge won't be vital. But I know you wouldn't want me to drown, after all.[62]

Bower managed to make a go of it for two more months, making yet another desperate plea for cash from Little, Brown in late August: "I have been hoping that I should not have to approach you again—I suppose that goes without being said. But when necessity reaches a certain danger point of urgency, something has to be done about it." She took some comfort in the fact that her struggles were widely shared: "We are all fighting through together and I am sure they simply could not pay more," she wrote of the magazines that now paid her a fraction of her old rates.[63] It was another two months before McIntyre heard from her again, in a letter written from the small fishing community of Depoe Bay, Oregon. "As to my being away up here," she explained, "I brought my husband up to the forest and sea for which he has been pining. We both like it very much and may be here for some time. I find that I am doing better work here and doing it much more easily than in the city."[64] Bower paints the move as a choice made for the sake of her husband, but one wonders if she and Bud were not among the millions of Americans left homeless by the Great Depression.

7

"Don't Be Pious"

According to early settler accounts, Depoe Bay, Oregon, was named after in Indigenous man known to settlers as "Depot Charlie," a member of the Siletz Reservation who worked at the coastal depot where supplies for the reservation were delivered.[1] At some point, he adopted a version of the nickname, Charles Depoe, for use in settler records, and the bay he was identified with became Depoe Bay.[2] The nickname "Depot Charlie" obscured Charles Depoe's more authoritative role as an influential member of the confederation of seventeen tribes who were confined to the Siletz Reservation through a complex treaty process that began in 1851. It was more likely in this role that he became identified with the bay, overseeing the distribution of supplies to his people. He was also a tribal representative in talks with settler leaders that led to the 1875 forced removal of tribal people from coastal land. Set aside for the tribes in an earlier treaty, this land had become highly attractive to white settlers, miners, and loggers who subjected the Siletz Tribes to violent attacks until they were finally forced to relocate inland.[3]

When B. M. Bower arrived in Depoe Bay in the fall of 1931, the violent history of white settlement there had been obscured by a settler mythology of "progress," and Charles Depoe had been demoted to the status of laborer in the few historical accounts that acknowledged him at all. The town that had been established at the bay had become a popular summer retreat for wealthy Portlanders who could afford to buy or rent a second home by the sea. It was also a destination on a "loop" for Sunday drivers out for an excursion.[4] Bud's son-in-law, Dan Sheahan, who was married to Bud's daughter, Martha, owned an old fishing camp on the north point of the outer bay, overlooking the ocean and backed by the newly built Highway 101. When Bower and Bud arrived, the cabins were all rented, so they stayed in a tent for the first night. At first Bower had wanted to pitch the tent in a cove on the beach, but the rising tide made her realize that was a bad idea.[5]

Within a few days of arriving Bower described her idyllic surroundings in a letter to her cousin Lydia. The cabin stood on a bluff facing the ocean and was steps away from a steep but doable climb down to the cove—"just a little shut-in nook, sheltered from the wind and with the waves lapping a pebbly shore out front." Adjacent to Highway 101, the surrounding property was "almost bare of trees; just little groups of pines here and there, and a three-foot carpet of ferns. Across the highway the forest rises in a range of mountainous hills." Bower spent her first days there "prowling along the shore" and making herself a trail around the point. Blackberries were in season, sold in old lard buckets by local children. "Sounds like pies in the near future, doesn't it?" she wrote temptingly to Lydia.[6] After enjoying all of the conveniences the 1920s had to offer, Bower quickly adapted to her simple, three-room cabin, equipped with the necessities they had brought with them for their "camp outfit"—a two-burner "Kampkook" stove, camp chairs, and cots. Ever needful of her own space for writing, Bower "created a Bowerish study out of a mere shell of a place open to the rafters."[7] A map of the Depoe Bay site, hand-drawn from memory by Bower's granddaughter Kate Baird Anderson, who spent her early childhood there, indicates a "studio in the woods" across the highway and a quarter mile up the hill facing the property.[8]

In October Bower wrote to Little, Brown of her intention to stay in Depoe Bay. She reported having a good start on her fall novel *Rocking Arrow* and asked for the customary advance. "The financial situation remains about the same, except that the overhead here is so much smaller that I shall be able to recover from the losses of the past few years. I do need money, I am sorry to say, but a hundred dollars will see me through very nicely. If you can make this small final advance I am confident that I shall not have to lean on you any longer."[9] Bower assured her publisher that her new surroundings were both "secluded from petty distractions and stimulating to [her] best work," but with her sprawling new property to maintain, she still scrambled to finish the novels that kept the money coming in.[10] Bud's illness meant that Bower was not only the sole family breadwinner but also responsible for all "choring" save the dishes, a task Bud zealously oversaw: "How he hates to see me come in and dirty a lot. He's got me so scared I wash my own egg beater and food chopper, for fear my only husband will walk out on me."[11] Some relief came when Harry joined the household during the winter. He converted his Buick into a truck, loaded it up with Bower's belongings, and drove "through blizzards and drifts, coming over the mountain ranges," to join Bower and Bud in Depoe Bay. He made improvements to the property like lighting and walking paths, and he assumed many daily chores, making a "big difference to the old lady's feet, time and temper."[12]

When Bower submitted another incomplete manuscript to Little, Brown in December, McIntyre quickly determined that another six thousand words were owed and sent a terse telegram to this effect. Little, Brown itself was under pressure from Bower's British publisher Hodder & Stoughton, who, after the fiasco with *Dark Horse* earlier that year, now stipulated a minimum length of seventy thousand words.[13] Now well-practiced at gaslighting her publisher, Bower did not apologize for what was almost certainly a deliberate tactic to secure payment for an unfinished novel: "I am sure you will not mind my decision to rewrite and give fuller dramatic interest to the last part [of *Rocking Arrow*]. . . . But when one comes closer each day to the need of money, both for one's own requirements and for the alleviation of distress, the tendency to hurry is really too great a strain upon one's craftmanship."[14] By December 23, with the novel still incomplete, Bower sent Little, Brown a handwritten, apologetic letter citing unspecified delays, including "minor illness in the family" and promising that outstanding chapters would be sent after the Christmas rush.[15]

In *Rocking Arrow* Bower struck a balance between the cowboy novels that Little, Brown preferred from her as the book market became more and more uncertain and her own desire to write about topics that better reflected her surroundings and interests. As an Oregon newspaper would later describe her method, "Bower doesn't write synthetic western stuff, she goes to the locale she wants to use in her fiction and gets the color and atmosphere first hand."[16] Her publisher, however, was satisfied with the "synthetic" stuff. Bower compromised: although featuring familiar western characters and plots, *Rocking Arrow* connected those things to Bower's new context on the Pacific coast. The connection was not without a basis in Bower's own experience; her first and second husbands, Clayton Bower and Bertrand Sinclair, both moved to the Pacific coast for their livelihood after their stints as cowboys. Clayton worked in an Oregon cannery, and Bertrand was a freelance fisherman in British Columbia. Like Clayton and Bertrand, Chauncey Moore, the cowboy hero of *Rocking Arrow*, does not ride into the sunset when ranch work dries up. Instead of fishing, however, he tries his hand at gold mining in Alaska. The novel follows his efforts to return to the family ranch after he hears of his father's murder. His journey includes an unplanned stop along the coast of Oregon after his hired boat is shipwrecked, leaving him badly hurt and stranded. "Eventually he does reach home and straighten things out," Bower wrote in a letter to Little, Brown summarizing the novel.[17]

As Bower settled into life at Depoe Bay, she found herself on a writing treadmill. Compared to the thousands that she had received for serial rights in the 1920s, she now got about a hundred dollars per story—if she could sell them at all. This put more pressure than ever on her income from novels, which were more time-consuming to write and were also paying less and less. Meanwhile Bud's health continued to worsen, requiring "special treatment" for which Bower requested another advance from Little, Brown in May 1932.[18] These strains made their mark on her next novel *Trails Meet*, which embraced the mystery genre more fully than *Rocking Arrow*, along with the darker themes that mysteries enabled her to explore. Her increasingly conservative publisher was alarmed at Bower's latest departure from expectation, and in an unusual move wrote her a relatively detailed and blunt critique: "[*Trails Meet*] is not considered by our [in-house] readers to be one of your best stories. . . . The inclusion of a murder mystery in the novel is quite all right, and the working out of the plot is about as ingenious as the average of your stories. We do think, however, that the story lacks the humor that so frequently is found in your work and that has pleased your readers; in other words, it lacks somewhat what we call 'the Bower atmosphere.'"[19]

Bower's response to this critique was immediate and somewhat irate. After two years of successive losses, she had difficulty manufacturing humor on demand:

Murder, parental hate and jealousy, political rottenness—these things did not strike me as being particularly humorous. But I am still smiling over your letter, and the idea of your reader's disappointment that a murder mystery wasn't so very funny. . . . I have learned not to expect enthusiasm or even praise from my publishers, but to take it for granted that my work is acceptable or I should be told about it. It must be my sense of humor that impels me to believe your readers were absolutely unconscious of any bias in their reading. . . . How in the world could they be expected to like this story as well as Rocking Arrow? It is news to me that they even liked that one; or any other, for that matter.[20]

Depending on the sales of her novels to survive, Bower had little choice but to relent before long. In August, one month after the argument over *Trails Meet*, she announced that her next novel was returning to more familiar themes: "I have gone back to the old type of novel which you appear to like, and am writing a story of the homesteader in opposition to the cattleman." She found a way, however, to make this clichéd western theme speak to her own recent experience: "I feel you will like to have it now when people are turning back to the land for the answer to their economic problems."[21] No doubt Bower had in mind her own relocation from the movie lots and restaurants of Los Angeles to the relative wilderness of Depoe Bay.

Even though Bower was living from hand to mouth, she was still doing well by depression standards. While many displaced Americans lived in tent cities on the outskirts of town—dubbed "Hoovervilles" after the president whose policies were widely blamed for the ever-worsening depression—Bower had found a scenic refuge with access to beaches and forests and a burgeoning tourist industry. However reduced, her book payments enabled her to assume ownership of the property from Bud's son-in-law. "This is such a beautiful country," she wrote to Vine of her new home. "Not so full of people that one feels crowded. . . . It's well worth the effort of getting started. . . . There's lots of fishing, off the rocks, out in a boat, or up the rivers after trout. Berries galore— wild raspberries everywhere—and the first wild strawberries since I left Minnesota."[22] As she had done in Quincy and Sierra Madre, Bower opened her home to visitors. Among the first were Lydia Benson and her family, who came in the summer of 1932. The two families spent their days exploring the coastline, fishing, or perhaps harvesting berries, and their evenings around a fire in the cove. As summer drew to a close and Bower faced another winter in Depoe Bay, she reminisced about the reunion with her trusted confidante: "I went along and put the sun to bed beyond the skyline, and all the little fishing boats were loafing along and I thought of you folks rather lonesomely. The same old sea rolling in and washing over the tiny kelp forest on the rock below—you know just how it looks." She closed her reminiscence with a particularly vivid account of their last night together: "I was seeing the girls [probably Lydia's children] curled up by the log and hearing [a friend] sing the Old Fashioned Locket. . . . Well, that evening will stick in all our minds, I think. I'm so glad you folks came and helped make some unforgettable days and nights."[23]

Before long, the rest of Bower's adult children, along with various spouses and offspring, joined her in Depoe Bay, further casualties of the depression. Harry was joined by his new wife Daisy and their son Bobby, who took up residence in one of the North Point cabins. Roy had recently parted with Ruby and married socialite Helen Van Upp, younger sister of actress and screenwriter Virginia Van Upp.[24] When Roy lost his job as a machinist in Los Angeles, he acquired a boat, named it Cara Lou after his baby daughter, and brought his family to Depoe Bay. The family reunion was complete when Dele divorced Alex and joined the household with her daughter, Sara Kate, affectionately known as Sarky.[25]

The map of the property shows three separate dwellings: a two-story house on the west end occupied by Roy and Helen; Bower's three-room cabin, which she shared with Dele and Sara Kate; and another building comprised of a cabin—where Harry lived with his family—a cookhouse, and an outdoor garage with additional sleeping quarters attached. Photos show modest wood-framed buildings with low, sloping roofs that stood in a neat row and faced the bluffs on the south end of the peninsula. The amply spaced houses afforded each family a degree of privacy, with companionship just a few steps down the path connecting them. Made of gravel, the path was illuminated at night by overhead lights from the cabins, as well as yard lights that Harry installed.

Visitors by automobile turned off of the highway onto a backroad that led to the point of the peninsula. Those on foot were greeted by a rose arbor at the easternmost end of the gravel path, while drivers headed to a central driveway that led to the open garage. Bower named the property "Trails Meet" after the novel she wrote during her first year there. The name also captured the property's role for a family drawn together by the travails of the depression.

At Trails Meet, Bower's extended family of seven adults and three children lived semi-communally. Each family had their own cabin, complete with a kitchen and a bathroom, while a shared cookhouse allowed them to gather for meals, and the gravel path encouraged frequent visits. The local fishing and tourist industries helped support the family; Harry and Daisy sold fish to residents of the nearby valley. Roy fished, took tourists out on his boat, and made souvenirs—beach scenes made of plaster—to sell during tourist season.[26] Roy's wife, Helen, somehow managed to afford a maid—a vestige of the more glamorous life she had known in Los Angeles. "Aunt Helen was my idol . . . perfectly turned out," Kate Baird Anderson—Sara Kate—later remembered.[27] Family photos show an idyllic place for a child to grow up. Sara Kate is shown posing on the carved steps leading down to the cove, perched on the shore with her feet dangling in the ocean, pausing among the wildflowers for the perfect camera shot, or seated on a wicker bench with a tortoiseshell kitten on her lap. "A very good likeness," Bower wrote next to the latter photo, "showing her fat cheeks. Too bad it doesn't show how red they are. And her hair is still a true gold. Lovely child."[28]

Too sick to play a very active role in the household, Bud lurks in the background of Bower's letters. The move to Depoe Bay had been at least partly a response to Bud's declining health, and in the early days there, it appeared to be working. "He is perfectly contented here," Bower wrote to Lydia, "which he wasn't in [Los Angeles]. He doesn't get out any oftener, but sits by the fire with his Chesterfields, Western Story Magazine and his solitaire deck. He's quite a radio fan now and never misses Frank Watanabe, Amos n Andy, Bobrick Sisters and Cecil and Sally. Those four programs are as regular as meals in this camp."[29] As much as Bud preferred his new home by the sea, his health did not improve in the long term. By 1933 he was an invalid, although he refused to admit it. "His health is such that he may drop out at any time without warning. Heart, hardening of the arteries, a cardiac asthma that keeps him fighting for his breath with the least exertion—he doesn't realize his condition, cusses his 'asthma' and thinks that's all there is to it. For which I am thankful."[30]

Eventually Bud moved from Bower's cabin to his own room behind the garage where there would be no children to disturb him. There he could play cards and read his western magazines in peace. Although Bower dutifully accepted her role as caregiver to her ailing husband, her letters betray some signs of irritation with him, particularly his inability to "readjust" as Bower had to the changing times. In an unusually frank description of Bud, Bower wrote, "I can remember none who so clings to the old range ways and range atmosphere as does Bud Cowan. I don't know another who has so shut out the present and lives on his past." One of the few photos of Bud from this period corroborates Bower's view, showing him clad in a cowboy hat and boots, rope in hand. Bud's lack of self-awareness—manifested in his belief that she modeled her cowboy hero Chip after him—was a particular source of annoyance: "That is not true, and cannot be true because Chip is an altogether different type of man. . . . I have in the past, just to avoid embarrassment for Bud, said that Bud is *supposed* to be Chip, but usually added that it was merely an idea that people got without reason. Bud has always tried to believe it himself. He doesn't seem to see how unlike Chip he is."[31]

While Bud read his western magazines and played solitaire, the rest of the family adapted to life in Depoe Bay. The newly built village offered grocery stores, restaurants, electricity, and running water.[32] In place of the movies, plays, restaurants, and shopping that had formed the backdrop of Bower's life in Los Angeles and at its most prosperous, Depoe Bay offered a quieter existence, but it was the beauty salon that she missed the most: "I pile on the cream and use the Fairystone every morning, because I go around bareheaded all the time. So I haven't tanned or gone leathery, but I won't mention wrinkles. Sometimes I see plenty, then again they seem to disappear. . . . My vanity will just have to suffer."[33]

During tourist season, the area teemed with summer visitors who rented cabins or pitched tents at the local campground, Pirates Cove. In addition to deep-sea fishing, they came to see the rugged shoreline carved with caves, spouts, and an underground lake. If they were lucky, they might catch sight of a whale in the bay. Aside from fishing, the town's main attraction was its aquarium, which was financed by town boosters to take advantage of traffic on the newly built Highway 101. World class at the time, the aquarium featured seals, octopuses, squid, crabs, and dozens of fish species, many of which were brought in by local fishermen.[34] Bower's photo album included obligatory snaps from most of these sites. Photos also show Bower and her guests enjoying a community fish fry, milling around a boat in the harbor, and rowing in the bay. They may have attended the fish races held in August 1934. A local paper described the bizarre event: the fish were turned "loose in the water with toy balloons tied to them to mark their course. . . . Then [spectators] bet on them—betting seeming to be the principal reason for holding races. . . . It ought to be rather hard to 'fix' a fish race—which is more than can be said for a lot of other kinds."[35]

Bower's steady stream of visitors included Roy's sister-in-law, Virginia Van Upp, accompanied by her seven-year-old daughter Gay, who visited in the summer of 1934. They were driven by a Black chauffeur whose presence raised some eyebrows in Bower's white settler family. "You asked where the [Black] driver stayed when Virginia was here," Bower wrote to Vine. "Well, he had a room at Crawford's. Depoe Bay was very nice to him, too."[36] Gay appears in Bower's photo album fashionably dressed in a sailor suit and ribboned hair. She and Sara Kate were close in age and, if family photos are any indication, spent much of their time together; indeed, Sara Kate later misremembered Gay as Roy's daughter rather than a visitor. Gay would go on to become an actress, appearing in several films in the forties and early fifties.[37]

Paul Eldredge, the self-identified "devoted fan" who had followed Bower to Nevada in the twenties, also visited Depoe Bay. He does not appear in family photos, but traces of his visit survive in the notes he likely took while accompanying Bower on a road trip to Portland.[38] One can imagine the conversation wander as the travelers admired the passing Oregon countryside. Someone remarked on a customer at a roadside melon stand: "Apropos of nothing, I liked the way that man lifted up and smelled that melon." Bower offered Paul, an aspiring writer, professional advice: "Watch for the flavor of words. I see the whole history of words, sometimes, slang words." She likened Paul's teaching job to Roy's latest business venture selling mountain spring water, which had emerged as a popular ingredient in beer: "Your success in life is inevitable if you carry on. You are writing professional stories now. Your teaching is for you what Roy's mountain spring water is for him. A means to an end." They gossiped about acquaintances and public figures. Nils Chrisander, with whom Bower had collaborated on his ill-fated biography, was "European enough to think that his presence is pay enough for the food and lodging he accepts." They weighed in on the scandal created when author Edna Ferber insulted oil magnate Waite Philips, calling his house "a combination of the Palace of Versailles and the Grand Central Station."[39] Philips "asked for it," Bower averred. Western author Henry Knibbs was pronounced "a little boy playing cowboy. Window-shopping in the West." Bower and Bud traded banter about some unnamed acquaintance: "Before he came to Wyoming, he had been a gentleman," said Bud, to which Bower replied, "That's quite an accusation. Can you prove that statement? Libelous."

Bower reflected on her estrangement from Christian Science, calling it, "Popery, Mummery." "I no longer lay my hands on my knees. And I feel just as close to the living heart of all things as I ever did before and not half so scared. Scared that I'd missed something."

On that trip Bower also shared a decision she had made about her writing: "I have decided to become a craftsman of western stories. I'm going to give the market what it wants. I've been trying to sell my ideals. I'll pocket them and sell what sells." Bower had no doubt been pressured into this decision by the conditions of the depression, which left her providing for her three adult children and their families on a drastically reduced income. Despite threatening Little, Brown that "there may be no more Bower books" because "there isn't enough in it," she had no choice but to carry on.[40] Beginning in early 1933 with *The Whoop-Up Trail*, she wrote a string of Flying U novels that she continued to trade for up-front cash. She no longer promised to end the practice of payment in advance. "I had hoped this would not be necessary, both for my sake and for yours," she wrote to Little, Brown upon requesting yet another advance, "but I have assumed the care of dependents who must be fed and sheltered, and I have no resources."[41] Bower also conceded to the increasing demand for violence in westerns, although she tried to preserve historical authenticity by setting novels such as *The Whoop-Up Trail* "in the earlier, more violent days when the sharp action so much in demand today is in harmony with the times."[42] In the fall of 1933 she followed up *The Whoop-Up Trail* with a sequel, *The Flying U Strikes*. The two novels depict the early settlement of the Flying U ranch in northern Montana, taking on subjects that Bower eschewed or satirized in her earliest novels—cattle rustling and vigilante violence—and emphasizing the role of the cowboy hero. Excerpts from both novels were serialized in *West*, which marketed western fiction in far less nuanced ways than had *The Popular*, featuring a gun-slinging cowboy on virtually every cover.[43] For all of her relenting to perceived demands of the marketplace, her payments continued to slide; she was paid only $1,500 for *The Flying U Strikes*. Equivalent to about $33,000 today, it would certainly pay the bills, but it was a far cry from the substantial sums Bower earned in the 1920s.[44]

After submitting *The Flying U Strikes* in late 1933, Bower continued to exclusively write westerns, although her next novel was not about Chip. "I thought I had better let him rest for a while," she explained to McIntyre.[45] Instead Bower reworked old material: *The Haunted Hills*, completed in December 1933, and *The Dry Ridge Gang*, completed in May 1934. Both were based on early short stories featuring the tenderfoot theme. She wrote one more Flying U novel in the summer of 1934; in *Trouble Rides the Wind*, Chip becomes entangled in what he thinks is a murder plot overheard at the local saloon.

With the spate of new Flying U novels, the Bower name became more closely associated than ever with the fictional ranch and its central character, Chip. Bower found herself dispelling myths about the origins of the ranch and its characters and even doubts about her authorship. One such inquiry came from Byron Crane, supervisor of the Federal Writers' Project for Montana, who asked Bower to identify the ranch upon which the Flying U was based, presumably so he could include that information in a Montana guidebook to be published under the program. Bower replied, "There has been almost as much fiction going about the country concerning my stories as has ever been written into them. I have heard rumors of other individuals who were 'B. M. Bower, who wrote the Flying U stories'; I have known of a dozen or more 'original Chip of the Flying U' men. I have heard of men who 'worked with the Happy Family' and know them well: and yes—I have been told to my face exactly where my Flying U ranch is located. . . . I'm terribly sorry, Mr. Crane, but please believe the author, who should know. *There is no original Flying U Ranch* such as I described in all of my stories. I wish there were."[46] Bower was especially wary of Bud's claims to be the basis for Chip. When Guy Weadick proposed to write an article about Bud for *West* magazine, Bower asked him to leave her out of it, lest the myth be perpetuated.[47] "Readers who know Bud could not help wondering how the author shot so wide of the mark in depicting the character, so it is best not given the permanence of print."[48]

Bower relied heavily on repurposed plots from early short stories for much of her output in the 1930s, sometimes producing an entire novel in a few weeks in order to meet unexpected expenses. "In emergency I did this in five weeks—with interruptions," Bower noted in her manuscript record for *Five Furies of Leaning Ladder*, completed in November of 1934. "Perfect copy—typing it myself." The "five furies" of the title are five daughters of a rancher implicated in a rustling scheme. Bower managed to follow this novel up with an original story titled *Shadow Mountain* about a conflict between cowboys and sheepherders. With very little left to lose, Bower based her next novel *The North Wind Do Blow* on her own experience as a teen-aged schoolteacher in late-nineteenth-century Montana. Little, Brown refused to pay for it, however, unless the recently published *Shadow Mountain* sold adequately. "Well, I don't eat much, thank goodness," Bower confided to Vine in a letter from August 1935 on this latest disappointment.[49] When she was eventually paid $1,400 for *The North Wind Do Blow* it was a new low.

Her many struggles aside, Bower did manage to carve out a fulfilling life for herself, even in her greatly reduced circumstances. She took interest in developments in Depoe Bay like the new restaurant and "novelty store" under construction, local property sales, and the comings and goings of local residents. A lover of all means of mobility, from horses to automobiles, Bower kept tabs on the boats in the harbor, sharing their changes of ownership and paint colors in the same letter to Vine: "The 'Pirate' boat is painted aluminum—Pirate no longer. And the Pauline has been sold again, and has a white coat—same old snout though."[50] The Bower home became an economic hub for the community when Dele's new husband, C. Verne Newman, started a factory there, making "sea witches"—baubles fashioned out of mussel shells and sold to tourists. During the tourist season the factory employed a dozen young women and could produce up to a thousand sea witches a day.[51] Harry had also parted from Daisy and remarried in 1934 to seventeen-year-old Hazel Latrelle Powell.[52] They and their baby son, Billy, joined the Bower household.

Bower continued the Muzzy tradition of community engagement and still enjoyed a good road trip. The letter to Vine describes in detail an excursion Bower took with a friend to participate in a meeting of the Townsend Club, an organization founded to advocate for a national seniors' pension plan. Roosevelt was due to sign the Social Security

Act on August 14, 1935, just two weeks after the letter is dated. The two women planned to take a side trip from Seaside, where the meeting would be held, to Astoria. Always one to take advantage of the opportunity to make an errand into an outing, Bower ended up spending an entire week in Astoria, writing, "Sorta hating to leave. . . . We stayed in what they call Finntown, down among the Fin fishermen and in a Finnish hotel (for both of us, $4.00 for the week!)."

The trip to Astoria took Bower within a short drive of Westport—at that time a cannery town on the Columbia River—where her first husband, Clayton, had lived shortly after the divorce. Indeed Clayton still lived nearby in Grays Harbor, Washington, with his second wife and two children.[53] Bower knew this "but couldn't even scare up any interest in the fact." Nonetheless she drove the twenty miles to see where her estranged daughter had lived before moving to Australia. "I will say that a more godforsaken spot I never saw. A scattered village of Oregon crackerboxes in a constipated growth of stunted timber, and the rest sand dunes. . . . Westport is on a two-mile long spit of sand possibly a mile wide, though I doubt it. So low I'd be afraid a good healthy sea would wash over it. I never saw a more depressing place."[54]

Bower's community involvement extended to activism on behalf of Oregon fishermen, who, in 1935, protested the low pay they were receiving from the canneries. On the same trip to Astoria, Bower had been enlisted by Roy to attend a meeting of the Pacific Coast Fishermen's Union; Roy appointed her a "Troller's helper" to get her a union membership. She embraced the opportunity to not only support her beloved son but to immerse herself in a new environment and gather "grist for [her] story mill." "I sat in with a hundred Finnish trollers and told them all about [efforts to break the strike in Depoe Bay]. . . . I got a great kick out of it," Bower wrote of the Finnish, Norwegian, and Swedish fishermen who dominated the union meetings and gave her the "inside dope on lots of things. . . . All told, we had a glorious time, and I see where I am due to write fishing stories for awhile. The way material rolled in upon me, I never will get it all in one book, I know that."[55] At the time, she was working on a book about fishermen in the Pacific Northwest called *The Trollers*, with illustrations by Roy.

His paintings of scenes around Depoe Bay, including a troller at sea, a boathouse, and a view of the bridge from the harbor, are still family heirlooms. Little, Brown, however, deemed that the novel strayed too far afield from Bower's usual subject matter, and it was never published.

Family oral history holds that Bower contributed to the Depoe Bay community in more iniquitous ways—namely by facilitating the supply of contraband alcohol to the community. The only documentation to corroborate this story is a photograph in Bower's album with the caption "Place of Plenty Booze" in Bower's handwriting. The photo documents a cache of alcohol that had washed up in one of the coves near Depoe Bay. Notes accompanying the photo explain that the liquor had appeared the morning after a suspicious boat passing through the area had capsized. If Bower had anything to do with the mysterious shipment, her notes make no allusion to this. The story of Bower's rumrunning may be a distortion of this event, or Bower's notes on the photo may conceal a more nefarious truth.

Tragedy struck just as Bower became established in her new home, and it struck where she was most vulnerable. She had made little effort to conceal the fact that Roy was her favorite child.[56] He was the child Bower chose to take with her when she left Clayton for Bertrand all those years ago, and the two were rarely apart thereafter. Whereas Harry appears in her letters primarily as a doer of odd jobs, from installing a new office in Sierra Madre to clearing the property at Depoe Bay, Roy is a confidant and collaborator. They shared the same fascination with new technologies of the day like air travel and electricity, and both were artistically inclined. When Bower divorced Bertrand Sinclair and moved to Bliss, Idaho, she took pains to have Roy join her, promising him a new saddle horse as an enticement. Roy and his first wife, Kitty, lived with Bower at the Pocket ranch in Quincy; their son, Roy Jr., was born there, and Bower entrusted the ranch to Roy's care during her frequent absences. Bower took an interest in—and supported—Roy's aspirations as they continued to evolve. She likely financed his share in the flight school he co-founded in California. She encouraged Roy to try his hand as a writer, mentoring him through the process in late 1928, only to "release" him of it when she recognized that his heart wasn't in it.[57] When Bower moved to Depoe Bay, Roy was not far behind. Bower became a union activist on his behalf, enlisted him as an illustrator for her fishing stories, and set aside a space in the sea witch factory for Roy to make his own souvenirs for the tourist trade. Dele was also a constant presence in Bower's life, but she did not occupy Bower's attention the way Roy did.

On October 4, 1936, Roy Bower and fellow fisherman Jack Chambers set out in Roy's boat, the Cara Lou. They were looking for three Depoe Bay residents—Eugene McWilliams, his teenage son Walter, and Walter's friend Gene McLaughlin—who had gone fishing earlier that day. According to news reports, the weather turned, developing a dense fog and fifteen-foot breakers after McWilliams had left. Knowing that McWilliams's boat lacked a compass, Roy and Jack had gone to find them, focusing their search on the whistle buoy at the entrance to the bay, where they hoped to find McWilliams's boat tied.[58] "In the fast-falling dark [Roy and Jack] forged out into the heavy seas and reached the buoy, calling to the other boat to follow them in. The McWilliams boat cut loose [from the buoy where it had been tied] and started to follow the rescue craft. After they had passed through the line of breakers, the trio in the trailing boat saw a huge breaker strike the other boat in the stern and sweep it suddenly from view." McWilliams managed to return to the buoy, tie his boat, and wait out the storm until the next morning, when he returned to shore with the two boys, all unharmed. Roy and Jack did not return. Their bodies were found by the coastguard later that day: "Jack Chambers was found three miles off shore, drowned, his head down in a life preserver. Bower was found tangled in the trolling lines of the wrecked boat, his skull fractured."[59] As if to grasp the last trace of Roy's presence in the world, someone in the family—probably Bower herself—stood on the bluff and photographed the Cara Lou as the wrecked vessel was towed into the bay.[60]

The depth of Bower's trauma from Roy's sudden and unexpected death is perhaps most evident in the sparseness of her archive after the accident. From here on, her story can only be pieced together from just a handful of documents, photos, and newspaper articles. Newspaper announcements reveal that Roy was cremated in Los Angeles, where funeral services were held five days after the accident.[61] Helen and their daughter Cara Lou remained in Los Angeles, where Helen would be close to her sister, Virginia Van Upp. Heavily pregnant when Roy died, Helen would give birth to their daughter Cecelia on October 25, three weeks after Roy's death.[62]

After the funeral in Los Angeles, Roy's ashes were brought back to Depoe Bay for a marine ceremony and interment organized by Depoe Bay residents and the local fishermen's union, held on October 18, 1936. A fleet of boats left the bay with the lead boat, the "Robert H," carrying the ashes of Roy Bower and Jack Chambers, accompanied by B. M. Bower and the parents of Jack Chambers. The floating procession stopped in the approximate location where the men's lives were lost, about one and a half miles off of the entrance to the bay. The ashes were set on a rowboat salvaged from the wreck of the Cara Lou. As a fisherman-minister led prayers, the little boat was sunk.[63] "A dozen fishing craft, tall-masted and silent, stood by while fishermen of the coast paid last respects."[64] On November 15, about a month after the funeral, Bower was a guest of honor at a fisherman's banquet in nearby Coos Bay, where she was presented with a birthday cake—she would turn sixty-five on November 25—and a fountain pen. As Bower accepted the gift she told the attendees that "her current novel, a fishing story, will have no villains in it, because you are all angels."[65]

Somehow Bower managed to keep writing. On December 8, she submitted her fall book *Pirates of the Range* for Little, Brown. It was a lengthened version of a short novel originally written in 1906. Meanwhile, the Bower household on the north point of Depoe Bay gradually dispersed. Too preoccupied with her own grief to look after Bud, whose health continued to decline, Bower parted ways with him. In January of 1937, Bud's daughter, Martha, and her husband, Dan, drove him to Nevada, where Bud would live until his death in 1938.[66] Harry had also gone, according to Kate Baird Anderson's notes on the period. The loneliness of the household was alleviated somewhat when Dele and Kate came back from Montana. As she had done before, Dele made the visit permanent, divorcing Verne, who had a history of abuse—his first wife had divorced him for "cruelty"—and remaining with Bower in Depoe Bay.[67] There are few records of Bower's activities during the winter of 1937, save her manuscript records—which suggest she was not writing—and a written recollection of Kate Baird Anderson, who had been about seven years old at the time, that "Roy's death affected Bower deeply."[68]

The deaths of Roy and Jack also had local and even statewide implications. Most residents of Depoe Bay had some kind of ties to the close-knit fishing community. The deaths at sea of two of its members were a harsh reminder of the hazards that everyone faced. Compounding the tragic circumstances was the fact that Roy and Jack had died needlessly. The incident was widely reported in Oregon newspapers, and nearly every article highlighted the fact that the McWilliams vessel escaped the storm unscathed, making the deaths of their would-be rescuers all the more poignant and perhaps compelling local and state efforts to commemorate the two men so that others can "pay honest tribute to the sense of duty which inspired their needless sacrifice for the trio in distress who safely rode out the storm."[69] Citizens of Depoe Bay and nearby communities raised funds for the memorial while community leaders from Depoe Bay and Portland spearheaded the project. Adrien Voisin, a prominent Portland artist, was chosen to design the monument, and a former Oregon governor agreed to give an address and dedication at the unveiling ceremony.[70]

May 30, 1937, was a festive spring day along the coast of Oregon. Blooming rhododendron and the emergent red foliage of honeysuckle vines brightened the coastline. Volunteers had been busy decorating cemeteries with "a profusion of flowers" in observance of Decoration Day—now Memorial Day.[71] The weather was fine enough to draw crowds to Oregon beaches, if not into the water, chilled by a strong north wind. It was a fitting day to unveil the memorial dedicated to Roy Bower and Jack Chambers, which still stands on the shore near the entrance to Depoe Bay. Adrien Voisin's monument consists of two bronze plaques mounted upon an oblong, six-ton boulder quarried from Rocky Butte in Portland.[72] On the upper, larger plaque is a relief sculpture of a fishing troller tossed by rough seas. Below it, an inscription: "From this harbor—in storm—departed Roy Bower and Jack

Chambers, fisherman of the trolling fleet, October 4, 1936, on a mission of rescue." The lower, smaller plaque bears these unattributed lines: "It is not true. Life is not slain by death. The vast, immortal sea shall have her own, shall garner to her this expiring breath, shall reap where she has sewn." According to news reports, several hundred residents of Depoe Bay attended the dedication, straining to hear the ceremony above the din of the nearby highway, busy with holiday traffic.[73] The ceremony included an address by former Oregon Governor Ben W. Olcott, an original poem composed and read by Ben Hur Lampman, a song by Portland singer Clarence Tolman, and an address from pastor William Wallace Youngston.[74] "What a man does for himself dies with him," said Youngston. "What a man does for others and for the world is and remains immortal."[75]

On January 27, 1938, Roy Bower and Jack Chambers were awarded posthumous Carnegie bronze medals. Roy's medal, accompanied by an eighty-dollar monthly pension, was given to Helen Bower, now living in Los Angeles and working as a secretary to support her two young children. News of the honor was syndicated nationally, along with a photo of the vivacious Helen and her two children captioned, "Mother's burden lightened."[76]

Not long after the memorial for Roy and Jack, Bower emerged from seclusion. On July 14, 1937, she appeared before the deputy county clerk in Salem to witness the issuance of a marriage license for her brother Chip and Bella L. Belding, who was described in a newspaper article as a housekeeper. Chip, according to newspaper reports, was now a resident of Depoe Bay.[77] Having parted with his previous wife, Nettie, who had remarried in June, Chip had moved to Depoe Bay to be with his sister during a difficult time for both of them.[78] While tragedy had drawn some family members closer together, others drifted apart. Roy's daughters Cara Lou and Cecelia saw little of the Bower family after his death. By the time Sara Kate was grown, her cousins were strangers to her. The clerk who issued Chip and Bell's marriage license, Harland Judd, was "elated" to learn that Chip's witness was none other than "noted" western author B. M. Bower. Bower graciously promised to send Judd an autographed copy of her latest book, *The North Wind Do*

Blow. After receiving their license, Chip and Bella were married in a "simple but impressive ceremony . . . in the presence of a few intimate friends."[79]

In addition to Bower's appearance at Chip's wedding, family photos from 1937 show a visit to an elderly relative identified as Aunt Jane Newman, who lived in a log cabin on the east fork of the Boulder River in Montana. This was Bower's first visit to Montana—a place with painful associations for her—since her trip to the Chicago rodeo in 1924. It may have been that the recent death of her son had spurred Bower to reconnect with other family members before it was too late, even if it meant a return to depressing territory. One photograph shows Bower and Jane posing together against a typical Montana backdrop of pasture, rail fences, evergreens, mountains, and open sky. In another photograph taken against the same backdrop, Kate stands next to a barbed wire fence, smiling dutifully. Someone had acquired color film for the occasion—a recent technology that would not be widely available until the 1950s. They used it to take a portrait of Kate holding a birthday cake adorned with a single candle, standing proudly in front of Jane's log cabin. The letter-sized portrait occupies pride of place in Bower's photo album, its colors vivid: Kate's blue dress, the pink cake, the pale blue sky, and the green vegetation—as if to symbolize a family's ability to see color again after months of grieving.[80]

In another sign of recovery, Bower began to write steadily again. She and Dele collaborated on a story that was completed in October but was never published. "Her plot and characterization [and] my style and technique," wrote Bower. Bower completed another short story in November, accepted by *Argosy*, and a novel for Little, Brown titled *The Wind Blows West* in December. But when Bower and Dele finished a day's writing, they faced a lonely existence. Formerly abuzz with the activity of three families and the laughter of several young children, two of the three cabins on the Bower property now stood empty. Without Roy and Harry to help, maintaining the property was also a daunting prospect for the little family.

By early 1938 Bower, Dele, and Kate left the relative wilderness of Depoe Bay for an apartment in Los Angeles. As Bower had always done before, she made the best of yet another period of "readjustments" by taking the opportunity for a road trip along the West Coast and reconnecting with old friends. Always enthusiastic about the accomplishments of modern progress, she visited the Golden Gate Bridge in San Francisco, along with Dele, Kate, Chip, Bella, her old friend Virginia Van Upp, and Kate's old playmate, Virginia's daughter Gay. The party drove across Golden Gate Bridge, newly opened the previous year, stopping for pictures on either side. On a trip to San Diego with family friend Paul Eldredge, Bower snapped photos of Dele, Kate, and Paul on Balboa Island and Kate posing in front of a full-sized replica of a Viking ship. It was a last hurrah before the family adjusted to apartment living in suburban Los Angeles.

After living on a spacious property overlooking the Pacific Ocean, Bower, Dele, and Kate now shared a few rooms on a quiet suburban street. There are relatively few documents from this period, but a comparison of the photos from Los Angeles and Depoe Bay suggests the general lifestyle change that the family experienced. Photos from Depoe Bay depict candid moments of outdoor activity: Roy by his sailboat, Kate posing during a break in an otherwise busy day outdoors, Bud showing off his roping skills. Photos from Los Angeles, on the other hand, reflect a far more contained environment and less spontaneous lifestyle: family members and guests are assembled on the lawn in front of the apartment building, posing against a backdrop of tidy lawns, modest houses with picket-fenced yards, and an orderly row of telegraph wires overhead. In one photo Kate appears with her father, Alex Baird, whom she had not seen since she was a toddler. Alex wears a suit and tie as if he has taken time out of his workday to see his daughter. They hold hands and smile broadly, but they stand apart like acquaintances rather than father and daughter. In another photo Dele, Kate, and Bower's secretary, Dawn, kneel on the front lawn, flanked by two young men in suits. The smartly dressed party looks like they are about to embark on an outing to a film or some other urban amusement. Bower does not appear in photos from this period except for one photograph with her sister Vine. She is either behind the camera herself or busy writing in the apartment.

In Los Angeles, Bower became reenergized, at least briefly, taking on new projects and new attempts to widen her market. Her book income had continued to fall—she now received just $1,200 per manuscript—and she had been unable to gain a foothold in the few magazines that had survived the Great Depression. In hindsight Bower now realized that her focus on writing for the pulps had left her without a serial market when *The Popular* failed and the remaining western pulps became more violent and formulaic. As she wrote to New York literary agent Edith Burrows, "The smooth paper magazines did not know me—my market [the pulps] absorbed everything as fast as I could turn it out, and I fear I followed the line of least resistance. After the debacle in the magazine world my market was pretty well shot." Bower now blamed Little, Brown for leaving her without a reputation that could get her noticed by the slick magazines:

[Little, Brown has] wanted the public to believe B. M. Bower is a man, and therefore have suppressed me as much as possible. I have long called myself the number one skeleton in the Little, Brown closet. My sex has been against me there . . . And after thirty-five years it is still believed by the general public that B. M. Bower is a man. Yet, according to the publishers' statement, something around 2,500,00 Bower books have been sold since "Chip of the Flying U" was first published . . . and no one knows B. M. Bower. . . . Figure that out for yourself.[81]

Bower had also made contact with Edna Schley, a writer's agent who specialized in stories for motion pictures. Schley had agreed to not only handle the film rights for Bower's books but also help her find work as a screenwriter. Bower hoped that "with Bower books on the screen, with the inevitable publicity, the smooth magazines are going to know B. M. Bower."[82] This final attempt to recover her career met with little success. Bower was able to sell only the rights to the title of her novel *The Singing Hill* to actor and singer Gene Autry for $150. The hoped-for screenwriting jobs never materialized. With only her books to rely on, Bower continued to write two novels a year for Little,

Brown, producing four manuscripts between 1939 and 1940 despite her declining health. One of these, *Sweet Grass*, was original; Bower had remarkably written the 72,000-word novel in only fifteen days. The rest were reworked versions of early short fiction about the Happy Family cowboys of the Flying U ranch.

In between submitting manuscripts for meager checks from Little, Brown, Bower found time for a new writing project: a memoir of the Muzzy family's early years as a midwestern settler family. This project participated in a wider movement in the United States to preserve the memories of nineteenth-century American settlers, spurred by the profound shifts of the early twentieth century. Bower was among many settlers who had witnessed firsthand the rise of automobiles, electricity, mass media, and big-city life. Bower reached out to her older siblings, now in their eighties, to collect and record their memories of settler life. In response, Ella sent Bower a portrait of her four older sisters—Ella, Lite, Vine, and Rose—seated in a semicircle, clad in dark-colored dresses and round spectacles, hands folded on their laps. Ella wrote a brief note on the portrait: "The girls told me to send you this one where Aunts Lite and Vine look so resigned and satisfied. Mine looks so much like me. I'm ashamed of it."

A photograph shows Bower, Dele, and Vine standing in a yard on a sunny day, surrounded by flowers and foliage in what looks like the backyard of Bower's apartment building. Vine may well have shared some of her memories with Bower during this visit; she recalled her childhood—before Bower was born—as the youngest of four living on a rural homestead. Vine told Bower about the various mishaps encountered by farm children in search of amusement, including how she was chased up a tree by the family's tormented sheep and dumped in the creek off of a sled the children had hitched to a panicked calf.[83] It was a far different life than the one young Kate now led on an orderly suburban street in Los Angeles. Bower would not complete the planned memoir, although her efforts resulted in a family archive that her descendants—and historians—are fortunate to have.

For a woman in her late sixties who had recently lost a son and a husband, traded a home overlooking the sea for an apartment in the city, and was in declining health, 1938 and 1939 were remarkably productive years. Dele and family friend Paul Eldredge would later call this period of productivity "the Bower surge" and refer cryptically to the "philosophy" behind it.[84] While working on her own Bower biography, Dele wrote to Paul Eldredge, "I have solved the problem of keeping too personal situations and attitudes out of the entire thing. . . . Let the public who reads, wonder. It will do them good to ponder how Bower achieved some of her philosophy of her later books."[85] Paul agreed, replying, "I'm all for . . . not telling the reader of the source of the Bower surge. Let them find out for themselves where that optimism came from. . . . To reveal such truths would only confuse them."[86]

Perhaps the "truths" that Paul feared would confuse Bower readers had to do with Bower's affiliation with a new religious movement that had recently come to Los Angeles. Advertisements in California newspapers enticed depression-weary readers: "Don't be bound by the troubles of the world. Learn how to use your I AM power."[87] An estimated one million people, including Bower, were drawn to Guy and Edna Ballard's offer of "secret mental and healing powers."[88] Claiming to offer followers a means to transcend death and become "Ascendant," the Ballards held extravagantly staged meetings attended by thousands. According to one newspaper account of an I AM meeting, the Ballards used "a dazzling stage setting, ushers dressed in white, even to shoes, passing out little envelopes with the notation 'I AM, Love Gift' printed on the outside. Microphones amplified the weighty words of the speakers, also in shimmering white."[89] Although I AM was widely disparaged as a cult in the press and would become mired in a wire fraud court case in the early forties, Bower, after a decade of financial and personal loss, was receptive to its message that death was impermanent and individuals had the capacity—through certain forms of worship and ritual—to achieve healing and positive change in their lives. Moreover, I AM incorporated Bower's Christian background into its theology by teaching that Jesus was one of the "Ascendant." Kate Baird Anderson would later make note of the importance of I AM late in her grandmother's life: "Bower had a deeply spiritual side [and] belief in Divine Order, good effects of prayer, healing, etc. Very sincere. Sought harmony, positive actions in daily life, creation of 'good energy.' Believed in second sight, knowings."[90] On the reverse of a page of notes on *Man on Horseback*, the novel she was working on, Bower wrote an I AM affirmation: "Charge me with Harmony's power. Harmony with goddess of Liberty's power of Loyalty and the Light of the goddess of Light. Make me a radiating focus of Light, Loyalty, and Harmony, from now on."[91]

The Ballards' claims to know how to circumvent death were compromised when, in December 1939, Guy Ballard died a rather ordinary death from cardiovascular disease. Around that time, Bower herself was diagnosed with inoperable cancer. Paul Eldredge speculated that Ballard's death may have aggravated Bower's illness because she had "based much on the hopes [that Guy Ballard] held out."[92] With Dele working as a secretary and with a young child in the household, the family needed help, so Bower contacted Hazel Latrelle Bower, who was living in Burbank, California. Although Latrelle—she went by her middle name—and Harry had separated, Bower thought that her former daughter-in-law would make a good nurse, having raised her own siblings after her mother died when Latrelle was just thirteen. Latrelle and five-year-old Billy came to live with Bower, Dele, and Kate, receiving room and board in exchange for nursing and childcare.[93] By this time Bower was renting a small house on South Virgil Avenue, providing the additional room needed for the expanded household of five.[94]

During those final months of Bower's life in the spring and summer of 1940, while Dele worked days as a secretary for a literary agency and Latrelle tended to Bower and looked after the children, Latrelle became Bower's confidante. Bower told Latrelle stories about her past, and, as her son Billy—now Bill—grew older, Latrelle shared some of those stories with him. Bower told Latrelle about her first marriage to Clayton, confirming the suspicions of those who knew them that Bower had an affair with Bill Sinclair while he was living with them in the cabin on McNamara and Marlow's ranch. She said she had an affair with Zane Grey and would reconnoiter with him on his yacht. She told Latrelle she had helped supply the town of Depoe Bay with contraband alcohol.

Although he was very young, Bill would long remember the day Bower died. It was July 22, 1940. Hazel had told him to go outside to play and not to come in without permission. He saw an ambulance arriving, and after it had gone and he was allowed to return to the house, the sick room was empty. Bower was gone. The draft of her last novel lay unfinished on her desk. Her last words, according to Dele, were "don't be pious."[95] Bower's longtime fan and friend Paul Eldredge pondered their meaning: "Was it a recanting of a long-held philosophy or was it merely the momentary irritation enticed by some well-meant religious consolation proffered her at her moment of parting[?] Probably the latter."[96] Bower's funeral services would be conducted by a member of I AM, strong evidence that she kept her faith in the sect to the very end. But Bower had lived an unconventional life, and her last words, showing she had no regrets, may have advised her daughter to do the same.

After the funeral, held July 26, Bower was cremated in her favorite lavender dress. On August 4, Dele and Kate flew over Ventura Harbor in a chartered plane, where Bower's ashes were scattered over the ocean she loved—where her beloved Roy had also been buried.[97]

Articles reporting Bower's death rehashed old myths and invented new ones. The *Los Angeles Times* claimed it was Bower—not her publishers—who, "fearing her readers would not accept [western] writing from a woman, cloaked her sex behind initials." The same article erroneously attributed Bower's success as a western writer to "girlhood days on a rip-snortin' cattle ranch."[98] In describing Bower's fiction as "jam-packed . . . with rough tough action of the range," the article also aligned Bower with the violent formula that she had long resisted. One thing the *Los Angeles Times* did get right was Bower's contribution to the western genre at its very inception, positioning her and Owen Wister as "pace setters for the subsequent flood of western stories, the popularity of which still holds good today."

Afterword

There is an expression that the best writers are those who "stand the test of time" as if through a process of natural selection, like hardy plants. In fact, authors' reputations must be actively preserved. Documents need to be collected and kept safe in order to be pieced together by biographers, anthologizers, and scholars. Often it is the family members who play the most crucial role in this process. If they are not the first biographers, they are usually the ones who preserve the documents that future historians will rely on to do this work. Bower's legacy was compromised from the start when Charles MacLean of *The Popular* insisted on keeping her identity a secret. Further, Bower's tumultuous life involved many relocations and dislocations that resulted in the loss of most of the hundreds of letters she, an avid letter writer, wrote during her lifetime. Her death left an already fractured family in tatters, and Dele, a single mother of a twelve-year-old girl, lacked the luxury of time and space for writing a biography. In dire financial straits after Bower's death, Dele soon remarried. She and her new husband left California after the attack on Pearl Harbor in 1941, fearful that California could be the next target. They moved first to Oklahoma, where their son, Reed, was born, before settling in Arkansas. Of his childhood, Reed recalls, "Dad had a bad temper and couldn't hold a job so we had a meager existence—no electricity & running water. [Mom] was unhappy and as soon as she could land a decent job in Springfield she moved the family. They divorced shortly after that."[1]

As Dele gradually found her feet, she fought for Bower's legacy as best she could. She had managed to keep Bower's papers—at least the ones that had survived, including the diaries, a handful of letters, Bower's manuscript records, book contracts, and other materials. In 1963, twenty-three years after Bower's death, Dele finally felt settled enough to begin writing Bower's biography. She reached out to Paul Eldredge, now a creative writing instructor at the University of Nevada, Reno, for advice and support.[2] She contacted Bower's old publisher, Little, Brown, to gauge their interest in the project and received some encouragement. She tracked down some of Bower's old friends—including a neighbor of the Pocket ranch in Quincy, and Bower's Hollywood friend Blanche Lovern. By 1967 Dele managed to complete six chapters, three of which she sent to Little, Brown. When the publisher rejected the project, a disillusioned Dele set it aside and she may also have burned most of Bower's diaries in frustration, but she could not completely abandon the project.[3]

One day in 1971, when Dele was working as an administrator for the Department of Anthropology at the University of Missouri, she attended a party held in conjunction with an academic conference. She fell into a conversation with someone who had just acquired a first edition of *Chip of the Flying U.* "I said very casually . . . oh yes, that was my mother's first book—and then I became the celebrity of the evening . . . and once more the embers were stirred up about the biography." The encounter, and others like it, goaded Dele. "Why does this keep bugging me?" she wrote to Paul. "It's almost like a daemon to be exorcised, but it couldn't be that[.] I have held to the premise that I need assistance, physically, and financially on this—and all I get is esoteric promptings, and continual references from out of the blue from complete strangers who are overcome at the thought of speaking to the very daughter of B. M. Bower."[4] Not long after Dele wrote this letter, she was contacted by Orrin Engen about a biography of Bower he was working on for his master's thesis. At first Dele was wary of an outsider profiting from Bower's life after all of the obstacles her own biography had faced, but Engen earned her trust, and Dele supported his work—a chapbook on Bower produced as part of the Twain Western Writers series.[5]

Engen's book provided only a brief sketch of Bower's life, leaving open the need for a more fulsome biography. After Dele's death in 1993, Sara

Kate—now Kate Baird Anderson—took on this task. She conducted further research at a time when this time-consuming work was done by telephone or mail. She contacted librarians and archivists in Montana, California, and elsewhere. She read widely on western American history and culture. She found an archeologist to survey the site of El Picacho Mine—now a nuclear test site—and compile a report. Kate managed to write four chapters of a biography but faced many of the same obstacles that Dele did, especially the lack of time and space for writing. The biography remained unfinished when Kate died in 2006.

Not long after Kate's death, her younger half brother and Dele's son, Reed Doke, compiled and organized the archive, and he set out to find a biographer for Bower. One of Reed's emails to western literature scholars was forwarded to me by a colleague who knew I was interested in Bower. Born and raised in Alberta, Canada, which borders on Montana, I knew something of the West that Bower wrote about, but I was a stranger to her family. I did, however, have access to the resources that both Dele and Kate had lacked: academic training in research and writing, grant money to pay for research travel, and an academic position that actually paid me to write. Reed generously opened his home to me, and I spent several weeks poring over the archives that Dele, Kate, and Reed had so carefully collected and preserved.

This biography could not have been written without the hard work of Bower's descendants. They always knew that Bower's contribution to American literature was important and should be remembered and that readers for years to come would be fascinated by her rich and storied life.

NOTES

1. AN UNBEARABLE SERVITUDE

1. B. M. Bower, letter to the editor, 181.
2. For traditional tribal and territorial designations, I have consulted the Indigenous-led mapping resource *Native Land*, by Native Land Digital, https://native-land.ca/, July 12, 2022. Any errors in designations are my own.
3. Dele Newman Doke, "Break Your Own Trail" (unpublished biography of B. M. Bower), 19, BMB.
4. D. N. Doke, "Break Your Own Trail," 22, BMB.
5. D. N. Doke, "Break Your Own Trail," 16, BMB.
6. D. N. Doke, "Break Your Own Trail," 18, BMB.
7. Unless otherwise noted, my history of the Muzzy family is based on Kate Baird Anderson's unpublished biography of B. M. Bower, "The Skeleton in the Closet," chap. 2, BMB.
8. D. N. Doke, "Break Your Own Trail," 41, BMB.
9. D. N. Doke, "Break Your Own Trail," 42–43, BMB.
10. B. M. Bower, letter to the editor.
11. "Two Great Falls Authors of National Fame," *Great Falls (MT) Tribune*, December 16, 1906.
12. "The Strike of the Dishpan Brigade" is reprinted in D. N. Doke, "Break Your Own Trail," 49–64, BMB.
13. D. N. Doke, "Break Your Own Trail," 45, BMB.
14. Baird Anderson, "Skeleton in the Closet," chap. 2, BMB.
15. Bill Bower and Reed Doke, interview with author, April 7, 2010.
16. D. N. Doke, "Break Your Own Trail," 45, BMB.
17. Montana, County Marriages, 1865–1950, Clayton J. Bower and Bertha Muzzy, December 20, 1890, FamilySearch; original source: Marriage, Hel-

ena, Lewis and Clarke, Montana, various county courthouses, Montana, microfilm 1,906,338, Family History Library (FHL), Salt Lake City UT.

18. United States Census, 1900, Havre, Big Sandy Townships Havre town, Chouteau, Montana, enumeration district (ED) 190, sheet 2b, family 451, FamilySearch; original source: NARA microfilm publication T623; FHL microfilm 1,240,910.

19. Bill Bower and Reed Doke, interview, April 7, 2010.

20. Bold, *The Frontier Club*, 74.

21. Pauly, *Zane Grey*, 146.

22. Moore, *Cow Boys and Cattle Men*, 3–4.

23. Moore, *Cow Boys and Cattle Men*, 98–99.

24. Moore, *Cow Boys and Cattle Men*, 168–71.

25. Moore, *Cow Boys and Cattle Men*, 161.

26. H. H. Smith, *The War on Powder River*, 7–48.

27. Moore, *Cow Boys and Cattle Men*, 39–40.

28. Kate Baird Anderson, "Montana Chronology," BMB.

29. United States Census, 1900.

30. Moore, *Cow Boys and Cattle Men*, 162.

31. B. M. Bower to Eugene Cunningham, ca. 1935, quoted in Baird Anderson, "Skeleton in the Closet," BMB.

32. Bill Bower and Reed Doke, interview, April 7, 2010.

33. Moore, *Cow Boys and Cattle Men*, 65–66, 130–31.

34. Little, Brown to Bower, June 24, 1932, BMB.

35. Moore, *Cow Boys and Cattle Men*, 39–40.

36. Baird Anderson, "Skeleton in the Closet," chap. 7, BMB; Bill Bower and Reed Doke, interview, April 7, 2010.

37. B. M. Bower, *Lonesome Land*, 64. Citations refer to 1997 edition.

38. B. M. Bower, *Lonesome Land*, 239.

39. B. M. Bower, *Lonesome Land*, 242.

40. B. M. Bower, *Lonesome Land*, 231–32.

41. B. M. Bower to Cunningham.

42. B. M. Bower to Cunningham.

43. Hinnant and Hudson, "The Magazine Revolution."

44. Baird Anderson, "Skeleton in the Closet," chap. 7, BMB.

45. Unless otherwise noted, all references to Bower stories in this chapter are from B. M. Bower's Manuscript Record Books, BMB.

46. Montana Department of Public Instruction, *Biennial Report of the Superintendent*, https://archive.org/details/annualreportofau00mont/page/54/mode/2up.

47. B. M. Bower, "The Maid and the Money," 145–49.
48. G. C. Smith, "The Popular Magazine."
49. Jan Kilcup to Kate Baird Anderson, June 27, 1997, BMB.
50. Photographs, "Up a Stump," "In the Clearing," "Gathering the Windfalls," "A Pleasant Row in Puget Sound," August 1903, BMB.
51. Payne, *Owen Wister*, 125–58, 198.
52. Bold, *The Frontier Club*, 88; Payne, *Owen Wister*, 179–210.
53. Keller, *Pender Harbour Cowboy*, 26.
54. Doke, "Break Your Own Trail," 93–94, BMB.
55. Keller, *Pender Harbour Cowboy*, 13.
56. Keller, *Pender Harbour Cowboy*, 26.
57. According to Keller, Sinclair boarded with the Bowers in 1902–3; however, if Sinclair helped Bower with *Chip* (as Bower indicates in her letter to Weadick), it is more likely that he was with the Bowers during the winter of 1903–4, since *Chip* was completed in April 1904.
58. Bower to Guy Weadick, June 13, 1933, GW.
59. Keller, *Pender Harbour Cowboy*, 44.
60. B. M. Bower to Weadick.
61. B. M. Bower to Cunningham.
62. Keller, *Pender Harbour Cowboy*, 28.
63. Bill Bower and Reed Doke, interview, April 7, 2010.
64. Untitled photograph, ca. 1903, BMB.
65. "Literary Notes," *Anaconda (MT) Standard*, October 1, 1904.
66. Ted Olsen, "Books and Bookmen," *Casper (WY) Star-Tribune*, January 11, 1925.
67. B. M. Bower to Weadick.
68. Bertrand Sinclair to Claude Dowen, December 20, 1959, Montana Historical Society Research Center, SC 1349.
69. B. M. Bower to Byron Crane, March 1, 1937, BMB.
70. B. M. Bower, *Chip of the Flying U*, 21–22. Citations are from the 1995 edition.
71. B. M. Bower, *Chip of the Flying U*, 36–38.
72. B. M. Bower to Crane.
73. B. M. Bower to Weadick.
74. Keller, *Pender Harbour Cowboy*, 29.
75. Lamont, *Westerns*, 62–63.
76. Allmendinger, *The Cowboy*, 52, 67.
77. B. M. Bower, *The Happy Family*, 120. Citations are from the 1996 edition.
78. D. N. Doke, "Break Your Own Trail," 66, BMB.
79. D. N. Doke, "Break Your Own Trail," 72, BMB.

80. Baird Anderson, "Skeleton in the Closet," chap. 9, BMB.

81. Bill Bower and Reed Doke, interview, April 7, 2010.

82. Ivan Ross to Dele Newman Doke, November 9, 1972, BMB.

83. B. M. Bower, *Lonesome Land*, 278–79.

84. B. M. Bower to Edith Burrows, August 30, 1938, BMB.

85. Big Sandy resident Connie Green, quoting her grandmother Agnes Milz McNamara, 1996, in Baird Anderson, "Skeleton in the Closet," chap. 9; Dan Cushman, interview with Kate Baird Anderson, August 30, 1995, BMB.

86. Illinois State Archives, Illinois Death Index (Pre-1916), https://www.ilsos .gov/isavital/deathsrch.jsp, April 30, 2021.

87. Marriage Certificate, Bertha Muzzy Bower and Bertrand Sinclair, August 12, 1905, BMB; *Great Falls (MT) Tribune*, August 14, 1905.

88. Baird Anderson, "Skeleton in the Closet," chap. 9, BMB.

89. Bill Bower and Reed Doke, interview, April 7, 2010.

90. United States Census, 1910, Washington, Chehalis, Westport, ED 15, image 1 of 4, FamilySearch; original source: NARA microfilm publication T624.

91. Bill Bower and Reed Doke, interview, April 7, 2010; Baird Anderson, "Skeleton in the Closet," chap. 9, BMB.

92. Bold, *The Frontier Club*, 111–17.

93. Pauly, *Zane Grey*, 10.

2. A BRIEF AND STORMY PASSAGE

1. Furdell, "Great Falls, Montana," 169–70.

2. Advertisements, *Great Falls (MT) Tribune*, June 29, 1904.

3. "Two Great Falls Authors of National Fame," *Great Falls (MT) Tribune*, December 16, 1906.

4. Keller, *Pender Harbour Cowboy*, 46–49.

5. "The Happy Family Characters" typescript, probably prepared by Dele Newman Doke, ca. 1965, BMB.

6. Modernist Journals Project, "Smart Set," accessed May 13, 2021.

7. B. M. Bower, "The Long, Long Lane," 135.

8. B. M. Bower to Edith Burrows, August 30, 1938, BMB.

9. Photographs, Bower and Sinclair at Russell's studio, artwork on display, ca. 1905–7, BMB.

10. Peterson, *Charles M. Russell*, 9–27.

11. B. M. Bower to Little, Brown, October 14, 1912, LB.

12. Peterson, *Charles M. Russell*, 17.

13. "Two Great Falls Authors."

14. *Great Falls (MT) Tribune*, April 24, 1906.

15. B. M. Bower, "Guileful Peppagee Jim"; B. M. Bower, "The Maid and the Money," 145–49.

16. B. M. Bower to Little, Brown, February 23, 1912, BMB.

17. Lamont, *Westerns*, 125–54.

18. Graham, *Community and Class*, 14–15.

19. "Two Great Falls Authors."

20. "Mills are Shut Down," *Great Falls (MT) Tribune*, January 28, 1907; "Montana Beef Off to Market," *Great Falls (MT) Tribune*, August 16, 1907.

21. "The Worst in 20 Years," *Great Falls (MT) Tribune*, February 3, 1907.

22. Keller, *Pender Harbour Cowboy*, 55.

23. D. N. Doke, "Break Your Own Trail," 104, BMB.

24. D. N. Doke, "Break Your Own Trail," 102, BMB.

25. United States Census, 1910, California, Santa Cruz Ward 4, ED 129, image 35 of 42, FamilySearch; original source: NARA microfilm publication T624.

26. *Santa Cruz Evening News*, January 8, 1909.

27. D. N. Doke, "Break Your Own Trail," 102, BMB.

28. Keller, *Pender Harbour Cowboy*, 54–57.

29. "Wander Thirst Is Satisfied," *San Francisco Call*, August 24, 1904.

30. Emilie Girard to Dele Newman Doke, September 16, 1972, BMB.

31. Girard to D. N. Doke.

32. D. N. Doke, "Break Your Own Trail," 110, BMB.

33. D. N. Doke, "Break Your Own Trail," 106, BMB; Keller, *Pender Harbour Cowboy*, 57.

34. D. N. Doke, "Break Your Own Trail," 110, BMB.

35. D. N. Doke, "Break Your Own Trail," 107, BMB.

36. Photo album, BMB.

37. Girard to D. N. Doke.

38. United States Census, 1910, Chehalis, Westport, Washington, United States, ED 15, sheet 2B, family 49, Ancestry; original source: NARA microfilm publication T624.

39. Girard to D. N. Doke.

40. Photographs, Carmel Camp, 1910, BMB.

41. D. N. Doke, "Break Your Own Trail," 109, BMB.

42. Photograph, annotated by B. M. Bower, 1910, BMB.

43. Photograph, Bower's writing tent at Carmel Camp, 1910, BMB.

44. Keller, *Pender Harbour Cowboy*, 60–61.

45. Dele Newman Doke to Ivan Ross, November 14, 1972, BMB.

46. D. N. Doke, "Break Your Own Trail," 106–11, BMB.

47. Kate Baird Anderson, "Chronology" (1993), BMB.

48. Kate Baird Anderson to Faye Messinger, Monterey History and Art Association, October 4, 1999, BMB.

49. Other documents in the Bower archive show the second summer camp took place in the summer of 1910; Kate Baird Anderson to John Jakes, May 18, 2000, BMB.

50. Keller, *Pender Harbour Cowboy*, 62.

51. Keller, *Pender Harbour Cowboy*, 62.

3. A LODGE IN THE WILDERNESS

1. Bower is likely referring to people who sold food on the trains.

2. B. M. Bower to Roy Bower, November 23, 1911, BMB.

3. Fred R. Reed, "Bliss Now One of Best Towns in State," *Idaho Daily Statesman* (Boise), November 20, 1911.

4. Photographs, ca. 1911–12, BMB.

5. B. M. Bower to Little, Brown, June 6, 1912, BMB.

6. B. M. Bower to Little, Brown, February 23, 1912, LB.

7. Notation on photograph of Bliss Ranch, ca. 1911–12, BMB.

8. B. M. Bower, *Good Indian*. The title references a racist phrase variously attributed to Theodore Roosevelt and Philip Sheridan. See Dyer, *Theodore Roosevelt*, 86; and Brown, *Bury My Heart at Wounded Knee*, 170–72.

9. Heaton, *The Shoshone-Bannocks*, 19–90.

10. Little, Brown to B. M. Bower, February 7, 1912, LB.

11. B. M. Bower to Little, Brown, March 19, 2012, BMB.

12. B. M. Bower to Selig Polyscope, June 8, 2012, WS.

13. Photographs, BMB.

14. B. M. Bower to Little, Brown, October 21, 1912, BMB.

15. Little, Brown to B. M. Bower, October 18, 1912, LB.

16. B. M. Bower, *The Gringos*.

17. Little, Brown to B. M. Bower, May 15, 1913.

18. B. M. Bower to Alfred McIntyre, February 18, 1914.

19. "Deals with Missing," *Oakland Tribune*, September 14, 1913.

20. "Dash and Daring of '49," *Boston Globe*, October 18, 1913.

21. B. M. Bower to Little, Brown, October 24, 1913.

22. *Feather River Bulletin* (Quincy CA), October 9, 1913.

23. B. M. Bower to Little, Brown, October 24, 1913.

24. B. M. Bower to Little, Brown, October 24, 1913.

25. Entry #122, note in Bower's Manuscript Record Book, BMB.

26. B. M. Bower to McIntyre, January 24, 1914.

27. B. M. Bower to McIntyre, January 24, 1914.

28. Marvin Benson, interview with Dele Newman Doke, ca. 1968, BMB.
29. *Feather River Bulletin* (Quincy CA), June 18, 1914.
30. *Feather River Bulletin* (Quincy CA), April 30, 1914.
31. B. M. Bower to Little, Brown, November 19, 1912, BMB.
32. B. M. Bower to W. N. Selig, Selig Polyscope, January 23, 1915, MH.
33. Bill Bower and Reed Doke, interview with author, April 7, 2010.
34. Hallett, *Go West, Young Women!*, 117–23.
35. Hallett, *Go West, Young Women!*, 113.
36. Hallett, *Go West, Young Women!*, 110–53.
37. Hallett, *Go West, Young Women!*, 82–100.
38. Kate Baird Anderson, typed notes, 1997, BMB.
39. *Enid (OK) Daily Eagle*, September 5. 1909.
40. "Is Hardware Saleswoman," *Wichita Beacon*, April 22, 1912.
41. *Topeka Daily State Journal*, June 14, 1911.
42. *Wichita Daily Eagle*, May 28, 1915; *Los Angeles Herald*, March 8, 1915.
43. *Los Angeles Times*, May 13, 1915; Lovern, letter to the editor, 38–39.
44. "Goldie Colwell," IMDb, May 28, 2021, https://www.imdb.com/name/nm0173459/.
45. B. M. Bower to W. N. Selig, January 23, 1915, WS.
46. "Buck Connor, State Ranger," *El Paso Times*, June 4, 1916.
47. Dan Agler to Kate Baird Anderson, February 25, 1995, BMB.
48. Manuscript Record Books, BMB.
49. Bill Bower and Reed Doke, interview, April 7, 2010.
50. After the divorce, Bill Sinclair and his new wife had moved to British Columbia, Canada.
51. B. M. Bower, "Santa Claus on Strike," BMB.
52. Dele Newman Doke, handwritten notes, BMB.
53. B. M. Bower to Little, Brown, May 20, 1915, LB.
54. B. M. Bower to Little, Brown, November 1, 1915, LB.
55. "Weaver of Western Romances in Wreck," *San Francisco Chronicle*, September 17, 1915.
56. Photocopy of inscribed edition of *The Phantom Herd*, BMB.
57. B. M. Bower to McIntyre, ca. November 1915, LB.
58. B. M. Bower to Little, Brown, November 1, 1915, LB.
59. B. M. Bower to McIntyre, May 4, 1916, LB.
60. McIntyre to B. M. Bower, May 28, 1915, LB.
61. Little, Brown to B. M. Bower, June 20, 1916, LB.
62. McIntyre to B. M. Bower, November 12, 1915, LB.
63. B. M. Bower to McIntyre, November 29, 1916, LB.

64. Notice for sale of the Pocket, *Plumas (CA) National-Bulletin*, November 10 [or October 11], 1917, photocopy from Plumas County Museum, Quincy CA.

65. B. M. Bower to McIntyre, November 29, 1916, LB.

66. Linda Brennan, handwritten note, Plumas County Museum, March 23, 1995, BMB.

67. Bower is likely referring to white shirts brightened from boiling and bleaching, and hair grease used to achieve popular male hairstyles of the day.

68. Paul Eldredge to Dele Newman Doke, April 10, ca. 1971, BMB.

69. Plumas County Museum, unidentified newspaper clipping, September 14, 1916.

70. B. M. Bower to McIntyre, November 29, 1916, LB.

71. B. M. Bower to Lydia Benson, April 30, 1921, BMB.

72. "Bower Notes," typescript, ca. 1923, BMB.

73. B. M. Bower to Lydia Benson, April 30, 1921, BMB.

74. Blanche Lovern to Dele Newman Doke, April 12, 1967; July 28, 1967, BMB.

75. B. M. Bower to McIntyre, December 11, 1916.

76. "Authoress to Make Tour of Country," *Feather River Bulletin* (Quincy CA), March 15, 1917.

77. B. M. Bower to McIntyre, March 31, 1917, LB.

78. Selkirk, letter to the editor, 62.

79. Photograph of SMS cowboys, 1917, BMB.

80. "Lady Drove Up from Los Angeles to Quincy," *Feather River Bulletin* (Quincy CA), August 9, 1917.

81. B. M. Bower to Little, Brown, October 23, 1917, LB.

82. "Must Be Sold at Once!," *Plumas (CA) National-Bulletin*, October 17, 1917, photocopy from Plumas County Museum.

83. *Feather River Bulletin* (Quincy CA), December 13, 1917.

84. B. M. Bower to McIntyre, January 18, 1918, LB.

85. "Mrs. B.M. Sinclair Disposes of Ranch," *Feather River Bulletin* (Quincy CA), July 25, 1918.

86. "Pocket Ranch Being Improved," *Feather River Bulletin* (Quincy CA), September 2, 1920.

87. "Fire Destroys Pocket Ranch House Yesterday," *Plumas (CA) Independent*, June 5, 1924.

4. NATURE AT HER UNCANNY WORST

1. Little, Brown to B. M. Bower, January 29, 1918, BMB.

2. Little, Brown to B. M. Bower, January 17, 1920, BMB.

3. B. M. Bower to Alfred McIntyre, January 24, 1920, LB.

4. "Women's Press Club," *Los Angeles Times*, March 20, 1920; "Penwomen Honor Unknown War Hero," *Los Angeles Times*, November 20, 1921.

5. "Women's Press Club," *Los Angeles Times*, November 2, 1919.

6. *Los Angeles Times*, May 21, 1917.

7. Kate Baird Anderson to John Jakes, May 18, 2000, BMB.

8. B. M. Bower to Guy Weadick, June 13, 1933, GW.

9. B. M. Bower to Weadick.

10. Robert E. Cowan to Little, Brown, August 18, 1919, LB.

11. "Lodge Constructed in 1914 Acquired by Campfire Girls," *Los Angeles Times*, June 5, 1941.

12. B. M. Bower to McIntyre, June 27, 1919, LB.

13. B. M. Bower to McIntyre, July 24, 1919, LB.

14. B. M. Bower to McIntyre, October 21, 1919, LB.

15. "Santa Ana Licences," *Los Angeles Times*, November 6, 1919.

16. United States Census, 1920, California, Los Angeles Assembly District 72, ED 319, image 19–20 of 28, FamilySearch; original source: NARA microfilm publication T625.

17. B. M. Bower to McIntyre, February 19, 1922, LB.

18. B. M. Bower to McIntyre, January 24, 1920, LB.

19. B. M. Bower to McIntyre, December 9, 1919, LB.

20. B. M. Bower to Weadick.

21. B. M. Bower to McIntyre, January 24, 1920, LB.

22. B. M. Bower to Weadick.

23. B. M. Bower to McIntyre, May 7, 1920, LB.

24. *Nevada State Journal*, May 20, 1924.

25. B. M. Bower to McIntyre, May 7, 1920, LB.

26. B. M. Bower to McIntyre, November 30, 1920, LB.

27. *Los Angeles Times*, November 1, 1920.

28. Dobie, *Coronado's Children*.

29. B. M. Bower to McIntyre, May 7, 1920, LB.

30. B. M. Bower to McIntyre, May 25, 1920, LB.

31. B. M. Bower to McIntyre, May 7, 1920, LB.

32. B. M. Bower to McIntyre, November 30, 1920; July 6, 1921, LB.

33. B. M. Bower to McIntyre, April 10, 1921; July 6, 1921, LB.

34. B. M. Bower to McIntyre, September 24, 1920, LB.

35. B. M. Bower to McIntyre, August 7, 1921, LB.

36. B. M. Bower to McIntyre, February 19, 1922; December 15, 1923, LB.

37. Photographs, BMB.

38. Harold Drollinger, "An Archaeological Investigation of the Bower Cabin Site," May 2005, B1–B14, BMB.

39. Jan Kilcup to Kate Baird Anderson, November 13, 1995, BMB.

40. Bower to Agnes Johnson, December 28, 1923.

41. "Bower Notes," typescript, ca. 1922, BMB.

42. Photograph, "An Indian Visitor," 1921, BMB.

43. Bower to Agnes Johnson, December 28, 1923, BMB.

44. Paul Eldredge, "The Skeleton in the Closet," April 26, 1971, 11, BMB.

45. Eldredge, "The Skeleton in the Closet," 14.

46. Eldredge, "The Skeleton in the Closet," 13.

47. B. M. Bower to McIntyre, November 6, 1922, LB.

48. Eldredge, "The Skeleton in the Closet," 13.

49. B. M. Bower to McIntyre, December 13, 1922, LB.

50. B. M. Bower to McIntyre, April 12, 1922, LB.

51. McIntyre to Bower, April 18, 1922, LB.

52. Reed Doke, email to author, June 17, 2021.

53. B. M. Bower to McIntyre, February 19, 1922, LB.

54. McIntyre to Bower, March 31, 1922, LB.

55. B. M. Bower to McIntyre, April 12, 1922, LB.

56. Pauly, *Zane Grey*, 97.

57. *Los Angeles Times*, October 15, 1922.

58. Unidentified Nevada newspaper clipping, March 8, 1924, BMB.

59. Bower to McIntyre, April 12, 1922, LB.

60. McIntyre to Bower, April 18, 1922, LB.

61. Edith Anderson to Little, Brown, January 10, 1922, LB.

62. B. M. Bower to McIntyre, April 27, 1922, LB.

63. "Bower Notes," ca. 1922, BMB.

64. McIntyre to B. M. Bower, May 31, 1922, LB.

65. McIntyre to B. M. Bower, May 31, 1922, LB.

66. B. M. Bower to McIntyre, May 25, 1922, LB.

67. B. M. Bower to McIntyre, August 11, 1922, LB.

68. McIntyre to B. M. Bower, September 15, 1922, LB.

69. B. M. Bower to McIntyre, September 29, 1922, LB.

70. B. M. Bower to McIntyre, November 6, 1922, LB.

71. B. M. Bower to McIntyre, December 15, 1922, LB.

72. B. M. Bower to McIntyre, December 13, 1922, LB.

73. Herbert Jenkins to B. M. Bower, June 11, 1923, LB.

74. B. M. Bower to McIntyre, December 13, 1922, LB.

75. B. M. Bower to McIntyre, May 28, 1923, LB.
76. B. M. Bower to McIntyre, June 22, 1923, LB.
77. B. M. Bower to McIntyre, July 28, 1923, LB.
78. B. M. Bower to McIntyre, November 26, 1923, LB.
79. McIntyre to B. M. Bower, December 4, 1923, LB.
80. B. M. Bower to McIntyre, December 15, 1923, LB.
81. B. M. Bower to McIntyre, December 28, 1923, LB.
82. B. M. Bower to Agnes Johnson, December 28, 1923, BMB.
83. B. M. Bower to McIntyre, June 5, 1924, LB.
84. B. M. Bower to McIntyre, January 6, 1925, LB.
85. McIntyre to B. M. Bower, June 12, 1924, LB.
86. State Archives and Records, Gaol Inmates/Prisoners Photos, New South Wales, Australia: Record Search, National Archives of Australia, accessed June 14, 2021.
87. Harry Bower to Little, Brown, May 12, 1924, LB.
88. B. M. Bower to McIntyre, May 17, 1924, LB.
89. "Famous Author of Western Tales Here," *Nevada State Journal*, June 20, 1924.
90. Unidentified Las Vegas newspaper clipping, September 20, 1924, BMB.
91. "$50,000 Offered for Family Bible," *Santa Ana Daily Register*, November 19, 1926.
92. Edward Clarke, "Evidence Found Warrants Deep Probe of Science," *San Francisco Examiner*, August 17, 1924 [Bower's typescript], BMB.
93. Clarke, "Evidence Found."
94. Clarke, "Evidence Found."
95. B. M. Bower to McIntyre, April 6, 1925, LB.
96. Photograph, ca. 1924–25, BMB.
97. Alan LeBaron to B. M. Bower, February 17, 1925, BMB.
98. B. M. Bower, "Place of Sacrifice," typescript of article for *San Francisco Examiner*, ca. 1925, BMB.
99. B. M. Bower, "Place of Sacrifice."
100. B. M. Bower, "Place of Sacrifice."
101. B. M. Bower to McIntyre, December 2, 1925, LB.
102. McIntyre to B. M. Bower, November 28, 1925, LB.
103. B. M. Bower to McIntyre, December 2, 1925, LB.
104. McIntyre to B. M. Bower, December 9, 1925, LB.
105. Charles Agnew MacLean to Alfred McIntyre, July 25, 1925, LB.
106. Kilcup to Baird Anderson, November 13, 1995, BMB.
107. Photograph, BMB.

5. DAYS OF LITTLE THINGS

1. B. M. Bower to Alfred McIntyre, September 14, 1926, LB.
2. Little, Brown to B. M. Bower, April 26, 1926, LB.
3. B. M. Bower to McIntyre, October 2, 1926, LB.
4. Bill Bower and Reed Doke, interview with author, April 7, 2010.
5. B. M. Bower Diary, March 23, 1927 (typescript by Dele Newman Doke). Unless otherwise noted, this chapter's account of Bower's life from 1927 to 1929 is based on surviving fragments of typescript copies of her diary in the B. M. Bower archive. "BMB Diary (DND)" refers to the typescript prepared by Dele Newman Doke. "BMB Diary (BMB)" refers to the typescript prepared by B. M. Bower.
6. Pulp Magazines Project, Magazines in the Project Archive, June 22, 2021, www.pulpmags.org/magazines.html.
7. Based on comparison of the Consumer Price Index. See Williamson, "Seven Ways to Compute."
8. Keller, *Pender Harbour Cowboy*, 155.
9. BMB Diary (DND), April 20, 1927; "Bookfair to Be Held this Week," *Los Angeles Times*, March 13, 1927; "Authoress Fights Anti-Rodeo Bill," *Los Angeles Times*, October 28, 1928.
10. B. M. Bower to Little, Brown, May 14, 1927, LB.
11. B. M. Bower to McIntyre, June 27, 1919; January 24, 1920, LB.
12. BMB Diary (DND), March 21–22, 1927, BMB.
13. D. N. Doke notation in BMB Diary (DND), April 13, 1927, BMB.
14. BMB Diary (DND), February 17, 1928, BMB.
15. BMB Diary (DND), April 17, 1927, BMB.
16. New York, County Marriages, 1847–1848, 1908–1936, Harold Clayton Bower, March 13, 1923, Monroe, New York, FamilySearch; original source: county clerk offices from various counties, New York, FHL microfilm 831,353.
17. BMB Diary (DND), April 21, 1927, BMB.
18. Minnesota, U.S., Death Index, 1908–2017, Minneapolis, Minnesota Department of Health, Ancestry.
19. BMB Diary (DND), April 24, 1927, BMB.
20. BMB Diary (DND), May 4, 1927, BMB.
21. Arthur E. Foulkes, "Financial Reasons Bring Terre Haute Aero Club to Its End," *Tribune-Star* (Terre Haute IN), March 15, 2008, https://www.tribstar .com/news/local_news/financial-reasons-bring-terre-haute-aero-club-to-its -end/article_7dd43f15-ca19-5a9b-ba26-4973851e4871.html; Vigo County Public Library, "Dresser/Paul Cox Field," June 30, 2021, https://www.vigo .lib.in.us/spc/timeline/subject/historical.

22. BMB Diary (DND), July 9, 1927, BMB.

23. Thomas Fleming, "The Admiral Line," *Columbus Free Press*, April 22, 1998, Freepress, https://freepress.org/fleming/flemng31.html.

24. BMB Diary (DND), August 1, 1927, BMB.

25. BMB Diary (BMB), August 1, 1927, BMB.

26. BMB Diary (BMB), August 4, 1927, BMB.

27. Keller, *Pender Harbour Cowboy*, 91.

28. Canadian Traveller, "Pender Harbour: British Columbia's 'Venice of the North.'"

29. Merchant, "As Far as the Eye Can See," 224, 229.

30. BMB Diary (DND), August 8–9, 1927, BMB. The shíshálh Nation has endured, winning self-government in 1986, with a population of about two thousand. See British Columbia Assembly of First Nations, "Shishálh."

31. Keller, *Pender Harbour Cowboy*, 131.

32. BMB Diary (BMB), August 7, 1927, BMB.

33. Keller, *Pender Harbour Cowboy*, 128–34.

34. Keller, *Pender Harbour Cowboy*, 165. According to Keller, Ruth divorced Bill in 1926, but Bower's diary notes her presence at the Stopping Place in the summer of 1927.

35. Dele Newman Doke to Ivan Ross, November 3, 1972, BMB.

36. BMB Diary (DND), August 13–23, 1927, BMB.

37. "Soldiers Field Becomes Ranch Today for Rodeo," *Chicago Tribune*, August 14, 1927, 8.

38. "Chicago Rodeo Is Real World Championship," *Chicago Tribune*, August 18, 1927, 13.

39. B. M. Bower, *Rodeo*, 136–37.

40. Laegreid, "All-Girl Rodeo," 5.

41. BMB Diary (DND), August 23–25, 1927, BMB.

42. BMB Diary (DND), August 29, 1927, BMB.

43. "9 Champions Named as Chicago Rodeo Closes," *Illinois Pointer* (Riverdale), September 2, 1927.

44. BMB Diary (DND), August 31, 1927, BMB.

45. BMB Diary (DND), September 2–3, 1927, BMB.

46. BMB Diary (DND), September 6, 1927, BMB.

47. BMB Diary (BMB), September 5–6, 1927, BMB.

48. BMB Diary (DND), September 9–12, 1927, BMB.

6. READJUSTMENTS

1. BMB Diary (DND), September 15, 1927, BMB.

2. BMB Diary (BMB), September 23, 1927, BMB.

3. BMB Diary (BMB), October 8, 1927, BMB.

4. BMB Diary (BMB), December 15–24, 1927, BMB.

5. BMB Diary (BMB), December 24, 1927, BMB.

6. BMB Diary (BMB), December 31, 1927, BMB.

7. BMB Diary (DND), January 2, 1928, BMB.

8. BMB Diary (BMB), May 31, 1928, BMB.

9. BMB Diary (DND), January 15, 1928, BMB.

10. BMB Diary (DND), January 22, 1928, BMB.

11. B. M. Bower to Alfred McIntyre, January 14, 1928, LB; BMB Diary (DND), January 14, 1928, BMB. Bower's diary entry notes that she "finished all but the last chapter of *Rodeo*, and sent MS to Little, Brown." Her submission letter to McIntyre, written the same day, does not mention the missing chapter.

12. B. M. Bower to McIntyre, January 25, 1928, LB.

13. National Register of Historic Places, Hollywood Melrose Hotel, accessed June 25, 2021, https://npgallery.nps.gov/nrhp.

14. BMB Diary (DND), January 28, 1928, BMB.

15. BMB Diary (DND), February 2–March 2, 1928, BMB.

16. Jou, "Counting Calories."

17. Norma Gould Dance Studio advertisement, *Los Angeles Times*, March 11, 1928.

18. BMB Diary (DND), March 3, 1928, BMB.

19. Christian Science Board of Directors, "How Can I Be Healed?," Christian Science, 2021, https://www.christianscience.com/christian-healing-today/how-can-i-be-healed.

20. BMB Diary (DND), February 23, 1928, BMB.

21. BMB Diary (DND), February 28, 1928, BMB.

22. BMB Diary (BMB), February 28, 1928, BMB.

23. "Burbank Day Sunday at Belmont Country Club Above Roscoe," *Burbank (CA) Daily Evening Review*, March 29, 1928.

24. "Wistaria Fete Opens at Sierra Madre," *Evening Express* (Los Angeles), March 9, 1928; *Sierra Madre's Wistaria Fete*.

25. BMB Diary (BMB), September 23, 1927, BMB.

26. BMB Diary (BMB), January 9, 1928, BMB.

27. BMB Diary (BMB), March 20, 1928, BMB.

28. Pollack, "Timeline of the Disaster."

29. BMB Diary (DND), March 14, 1928, BMB.

30. BMB Diary (DND), March 17, 1928, BMB.

31. BMB Diary (BMB), March 28, 1928, BMB.

32. BMB Diary (BMB), April 28, 1928, BMB.

33. BMB Diary (DND), June 19, 1928, BMB.

34. BMB Diary (DND), June 14, 1928, BMB.

35. B. M. Bower to McIntyre, July 7, 1928, LB.

36. BMB Diary (DND), August 18, 1928, BMB.

37. G. C. Smith, "The Popular Magazine."

38. B. M. Bower, untitled (comments on death of Charles MacLean), 1928, BMB.

39. MacRae, director, *King of the Rodeo*, starring Hoot Gibson, 1929, https:// archive.org/details/Httparchive.orgKINGOFTHERODEO.

40. Bower to McIntyre, July 7, 1928, LB.

41. Little, Brown to Bower, July 12, 1928, LB.

42. Slide, *Early American Cinema*, 182.

43. Slide, *Early American Cinema*, 184.

44. "Voter Information Guide for 1928, General Election," UC Hastings Scholarship Repository, 1928, http://repository.uchastings.edu/ca_ballot_props/251.

45. "Animal Views on Rodeo Told," *Los Angeles Times*, October 21, 1928, 20.

46. "Parade of Protest to Take Place," *Los Angeles Times*, November 5, 1928.

47. BMB Diary (DND), October 4, 1928, BMB.

48. BMB Diary (DND), November 8, 1928, BMB.

49. BMB Diary (DND), November 10, 1928, BMB.

50. BMB Diary (BMB), December 16, 1928, BMB.

51. BMB Diary (DND), April 26, 1929, BMB.

52. B. M. Bower to McIntyre, November 1, 1929, LB.

53. B. M. Bower to McIntyre, July 24, 1930, LB.

54. B. M. Bower to McIntyre, April 26, 1930, LB.

55. McIntyre to B. M. Bower, July 10, 1930, LB.

56. B. M. Bower to McIntyre, July 16, 1930, LB.

57. B. M. Bower to McIntyre, July 16, 1930, LB.

58. B. M. Bower to McIntyre, November 10, 1930, LB.

59. Little, Brown to B. M. Bower, March 20, 1931, LB.

60. W. J. Knight to Hodder & Stoughton, May 1, 1931, LB. This letter to Bower's UK publisher was forwarded to Little, Brown.

61. Curtis Brown to Herbert Jenkins, May 27, 1931, LB.

62. B. M. Bower to McIntyre, June 17, 1931, LB.

63. B. M. Bower to McIntyre, August 17, 1931, LB.

64. B. M. Bower to McIntyre, October 27, 1931, LB.

7. "DON'T BE PIOUS"

1. "News and Comment," 365.

2. Robert DePoe Student Information Card, Carlisle Indian School Digital Resource Center, accessed July 12, 2021, http://carlisleindian.dickinson.edu /student_files/robert-depoe-student-information-card.

3. Schwartz, The Rogue River, 240–49; "Changing Federal Policy & Reduction of the Coast Reservation by Act of Congress, 1875," Confederated Tribes of Siletz Indians, accessed December 1, 2022, https://www.ctsi.nsn .us/changing-federal-policy-reduction-of-the-coast-reservation-by-act-of -congress-1875/.

4. Steve Mergler, "Beautiful, Captivating Loop Trip," *Oregon Statesman*, June 14, 1931.

5. B. M. Bower to Lydia Benson, September 5, 1931, BMB.

6. B. M. Bower to Lydia Benson, September 5, 1931, BMB.

7. B. M. Bower to Lydia Benson, January 28, 1932, BMB.

8. Kate Baird Anderson, hand-drawn map of Depoe Bay compound, BMB.

9. B. M. Bower to Alfred McIntyre, October 27, 1931, LB.

10. B. M. Bower to McIntyre, December 12, 1931, LB.

11. B. M. Bower to Lydia Benson, January 28, 1932, BMB.

12. B. M. Bower to Lydia Benson, January 28, 1932, BMB.

13. McIntyre to B. M. Bower, December 12, 1931, LB.

14. B. M. Bower to McIntyre, December 12, 1931, LB.

15. B. M. Bower to McIntyre, December 23, 1931, LB.

16. "Meet B.M. Bower, Tale Teller," *The World* (Coos Bay OR), November 17, 1936.

17. B. M. Bower to McIntyre, October 27, 1931, LB.

18. B. M. Bower to McIntyre, May 9, 1932, LB.

19. McIntyre to B. M. Bower, June 24, 1932, LB.

20. B. M. Bower to McIntyre, July 11, 1932, LB.

21. B. M. Bower to McIntyre, August 11, 1932, LB.

22. B. M. Bower to Vine (Lucy Lavinia Johnson [née Muzzy]), May 28, 1932, BMB.

23. B. M. Bower to Lydia Benson, August 29, 1932, BMB.

24. United States Census, 1920, Los Angeles Assembly District 72, ED 335, image 32 of 41, FamilySearch; original source: NARA microfilm publication T625.

25. Sara Kate would be known as Kate Baird Anderson in adulthood.

26. "Depoe Bay Gets Ready for Year," *Corvallis (OR) Gazette-Times*, April 17, 1935.

27. Kate Baird Anderson, "Information for the B. M. Bower Biography—1997," typed notes, BMB.

28. B. M. Bower, notation in photo album, BMB.

29. B. M. Bower to Lydia Benson, January 28, 1932, BMB.

30. B. M. Bower to Guy Weadick, June 13, 1933, GW.

31. B. M. Bower to Guy Weadick, June 13, 1933, GW.

32. Mrs. Blaine Hovey, "Coast Aquarium Is Described by Mrs. Blaine Hovey," *Eugene (OR) Guard*, July 28, 1935.

33. B. M. Bower to Lydia Benson, January 28, 1932, BMB.

34. Hovey, "Coast Aquarium."

35. *Klamath Falls (OR) Evening Herald*, August 8, 1934.

36. B. M. Bower to Vine Johnson, August 1, 1935, BMB.

37. Philip Scheuer, "First of 'Third Generation' Screen Careers Launched," *Los Angeles Times*, November 3, 1946; California, County Marriages, 1850–1952, Virginia A Van Upp in entry for Robert Marshall De Haven and Virginia Gay Nelson, 1947, FamilySearch. Gay's relation to Virginia Van Upp is uncertain. Scheuer identifies her as Virginia's granddaughter, but marriage records identify her as the daughter of Virginia Van Upp and Ralph Nelson. Gay's unplanned birth—to either Virginia or Helen Van Upp—may have been the subject of the convent reference in Bower's diary entry of January 22, 1928, BMB. See p. 105 in this volume.

38. "Notes Taken on a Trip to Portland from Depoe Bay," typescript attributed to Paul Eldredge, ca. 1932, BMB.

39. Wallis, *Art Deco Tulsa*, 9.

40. B. M. Bower to McIntyre, July 11, 1932, LB.

41. B. M. Bower to McIntyre, December 20, 1932, LB.

42. B. M. Bower to McIntyre, February 20, 1933, LB.

43. Stephensen-Payne, "The Western and Frontier Fiction Magazine Index."

44. Based on comparison of the Consumer Price Index. See Williamson, "Seven Ways to Compute."

45. B. M. Bower to McIntyre, October 10, 1933, LB.

46. B. M. Bower to Byron Crane, March 1, 1937, BMB.

47. The article about Bud was likely part of Weadick's series "Cowboys I Have Known," which ran in *West* from 1933 to 1936. See Stephensen-Payne, "The Western and Frontier Fiction Magazine Index."

48. B. M. Bower to Weadick, June 13, 1933, GW.

49. B. M. Bower to Vine Johnson, August 1, 1935, BMB.

50. B. M. Bower to Vine Johnson, August 1, 1935, BMB.

51. "Depoe Bay Gets Ready for the Year."

52. Washington, U.S., Marriage Records, 1854–2013, Washington State Archives, Olympia, Ancestry.

53. United States Census, 1930, Washington, Grays Harbor, Grayland, ED 30, image 5 of 10, FamilySearch; original source: NARA microfilm publication T626, 2002.
54. B. M. Bower to Vine Johnson, August 1, 1935, BMB.
55. B. M. Bower to Vine Johnson, August 1, 1935, BMB.
56. Bill Bower and Reed Doke, interview with author, April 7, 2010.
57. BMB Diary (DND), January 2, 1929, BMB.
58. "Two Fishermen Die Saving Two Others in Storm," *Sacramento Bee*, October 5, 1936.
59. Unidentified newspaper articles, scrapbook, 1938, BMB.
60. Photograph, "Towing 'Cara Lou' into Harbor after Roy's Death," October 5, 1936, BMB.
61. Pierce Brothers Funeral Services advertisement, "Funeral Services," *Los Angeles Evening Citizen* (Hollywood), October 9, 1936.
62. "Award to Hero's Family," *Minneapolis Star*, February 3, 1938.
63. "Joint Marine Funeral Will Honor Heroes," *Capital Journal* (Salem OR), October 15, 1936.
64. "Ashes of Heroes Received by Sea," *Capital Journal* (Salem OR), October 19, 1936.
65. "Electing Officers on Program for Fishermen Meet," *The World* (Coos Bay OR), November 16, 1936.
66. "Writers Mate Dies in Vegas," *Nevada State Journal* (Reno), July 7, 1938.
67. Oregon, U.S., State Divorces, 1925–1968, Oregon Center for Health Statistics, Portland, Divorce Records, 1925–1945, Ancestry.
68. Kate Baird Anderson, B. M. Bower Chronology, 1993, BMB.
69. "The Spirit of Youth," *Capital Journal* (Salem OR), May 31, 1937.
70. "Monolith to Depoe Heroes," *Capital Journal* (Salem OR), May 31, 1937.
71. "Beaches Attract Folk on Holiday," *Statesman Journal* (Salem OR), June 1, 1937.
72. "Monolith to Depoe Heroes."
73. "The Spirit of Youth."
74. *Statesman Journal* (Salem OR), April 16, 1937.
75. "Monolith to Depoe Heroes."
76. "Award to Hero's Family."
77. "Author Attests Wedding License," *Capital Journal* (Salem OR), July 15, 1937.
78. Oregon, U.S., State Marriages, 1906–1968, Oregon Center for Health Statistics, Portland, State Marriages, 1911–1945, Ancestry.
79. "Author Attests Wedding License."
80. Photographs, BMB.

81. B. M. Bower to Edith Burrows, August 30, 1938, BMB. Ellipses in original.
82. B. M. Bower to Burrows, August 30, 1938, BMB.
83. "Vine Remembers," recollections of Lucy Lavinia (Vine) Johnson [née Muzzy] as told to B. M. Bower, ca. 1938, BMB.
84. Paul Eldredge to Dele Newman Doke, November 16, 1967.
85. D. N. Doke to Eldredge, November 14, 1967, BMB.
86. Eldredge to D. N. Doke, November 16, 1967, BMB.
87. Church of the Ascended Masters advertisement, *Hollywood Citizen-News*, February 26, 1938.
88. Barrett, *Sects, 'Cults,' and Alternative*, 191; Church of the Ascended Masters advertisement.
89. Don S. Avery, "Pannings," *Siskiyou News* (Yreka CA), February 24, 1938.
90. Kate Baird Anderson, "Bower and I AM Movement," handwritten notes, ca. 1996, BMB.
91. B. M. Bower, handwritten notes, ca. 1939, BMB.
92. Eldredge to D. N. Doke, July 31, 1940, BMB.
93. Bill Bower and Reed Doke, interview, April 7, 2010.
94. United States Census, 1940, California, Los Angeles, Los Angeles Township, Los Angeles, Councilmanic District 4, 60–258 Los Angeles Township, Los Angeles City Councilmanic District 4 (Tract 102—part) in Assembly District 56, Barclay Arms Apartments, image 9 of 34, FamilySearch; original source: Sixteenth Census of the United States, 1940, NARA digital publication T627, Records of the Bureau of the Census, 1790–2007, RG 29, 2012.
95. Eldredge to D. N. Doke, March 16, 1963, BMB; Reed Doke, email message to author, July 25, 2021. Dele's son Reed Doke recalled, "Mom talked about Bower's 'don't be pious' statement many, many times as I was growing up."
96. Eldredge to D. N. Doke, March 16, 1963, BMB.
97. Unidentified clippings, notes, photographs, ca. 1940, BMB.
98. "B. M. Bower, Author of 68 Western Novels, Succumbs," *Los Angeles Times*, July 24, 1940.

AFTERWORD

1. Reed Doke, email to author, July 25, 2021.
2. Paul Eldredge to Dele Newman Doke, March 16, 1963, BMB.
3. Bill Bower and Reed Doke, interview with author, April 7, 2010.
4. D. N. Doke to Eldredge, March 24, 1971, BMB.
5. D. N. Doke to Eldredge, June 26, 1972, BMB.

BIBLIOGRAPHY

ARCHIVES

BMB. B. M. Bower Papers. Private collection of Reed Doke. Now on deposit at the Montana Historical Society (not yet catalogued at time of writing).

GW. B. M. Bower letter to Guy Weadick. Guy Weadick fonds, Glenbow Museum, Calgary, Alberta CA.

LB. Little, Brown and Company Records, 1810–1996. MS Am 3171. Houghton Library, Harvard University.

NARA. National Archives and Records Administration. Washington DC.

WS. William Selig Papers. Margaret Herrick Library, Academy of Motion Picture Arts and Sciences, Beverly Hills CA.

PUBLISHED WORKS

Allmendinger, Blake. *The Cowboy: Representations of Labor in an American Work Culture*. New York: Oxford University Press, 1992.

Barrett, David V. *Sects, 'Cults,' and Alternative Religions: A World Survey and Sourcebook*. London: Blandford, 1996.

Beaumont, Ronald C. "Sechelt Dictionary." Vancouver: University of British Columbia, 2011. https://doi.org/10.14288/1.0107947.

Bold, Christine. *The Frontier Club: Popular Westerns and Cultural Power, 1880–1924*. New York: Oxford University Press, 2013.

Bower, B. M. *The Adam Chasers*. Boston: Little, Brown, 1927.

———. "At the Grey Wolf's Den." *Ainslee's*, 1904.

———. *Cabin Fever*. Boston: Little, Brown, 1918.

———. *Casey Ryan*. Boston: Little, Brown, 1921.

———. *Chip of the Flying U*. Boston: Little, Brown, 1906; Lincoln: University of Nebraska Press, 1995.

———. *Cow-Country*. Boston: Little, Brown, 1921.

———. *Dark Horse*. Boston: Little, Brown, 1931.

———. *Desert Brew*. Boston: Little, Brown, 1924.

———. *The Dry Ridge Gang*. Boston: Little, Brown, 1935.

———. *The Eagle's Wing*. Boston: Little, Brown, 1924.

———. *Five Furies of Leaning Ladder*. Boston: Little, Brown, 1936.

———. *Flying U Ranch*. New York: G. W. Dillingham, 1914.

———. *The Flying U Strikes*. Boston: Little, Brown, 1934.

———. *Fool's Goal*. Boston: Little, Brown, 1930.

———. *Good Indian*. Boston: Little, Brown, 1912.

———. *The Gringos*. Boston: Little, Brown, 1913.

———. "Guileful Peppagee Jim." *Argonaut*, August 24, 1903.

———. *The Happy Family of the Flying U*. New York: G. W. Dillingham, 1910; Lincoln: University of Nebraska Press, 1996.

———. *The Haunted Hills*. Boston: Little, Brown, 1934.

———. *Hay-Wire*. Boston: Little, Brown, 1928.

———. *The Heritage of the Sioux*. Boston: Little, Brown, 1916.

———. *Jean of the Lazy A*. Boston: Little, Brown, 1915.

———. *Laughing Water*. Boston: Little, Brown, 1982.

———. Letter to the editor. *Adventure* (December 10, 1924): 181–83.

———. *Lonesome Land*. Boston: Little, Brown, 1912; Lincoln: University of Nebraska Press, 1997.

———. "The Long, Long Lane." *Smart Set* 20, no. 2 (October 1906): 134.

———. *The Long Loop*. Boston: Little, Brown, 1931.

———. *The Lookout Man*. Boston: Little, Brown, 1917.

———. "The Maid and the Money." *Ainslee's*, October 1903.

———. *Man on Horseback*. Boston: Little, Brown, 1940.

———. *Meadowlark Basin*. Boston: Little, Brown, 1925.

———. *The North Wind Do Blow*. Boston: Little, Brown, 1937.

———. *The Parowan Bonanza*. Boston: Little, Brown, 1923.

———. *The Phantom Herd*. Boston: Little, Brown, 1916.

———. *Pirates of the Range*. Boston: Little, Brown, 1937.

———. *Points West*. Boston: Little, Brown, 1928.

———. *The Ranch at the Wolverine*. Boston: Little, Brown, 1914.

———. *Rocking Arrow*. Boston: Little, Brown, 1932.

———. *Rodeo*. Toronto: McCelland and Stewart, 1929.

———. *Shadow Mountain*. Boston: Little, Brown, 1936.

———. *The Singing Hill*. Boston: Little, Brown, 1939.

———. *Skyrider*. Boston: Little, Brown, 1918.

———. *Starr, of the Desert*. Boston: Little, Brown, 1917.

———. *The Swallowfork Bulls*. Boston: Little, Brown, 1929.

———. *Sweet Grass*. Boston: Little, Brown, 1940.

———. *The Thunder Bird*. Boston: Little, Brown, 1919.

———. *Tiger Eye*. Boston: Little, Brown, 1930.

———. *Trails Meet*. Boston: Little, Brown, 1933.

———. *Trouble Rides the Wind*. Boston: Little, Brown, 1935.

———. *The Uphill Climb*. Boston: Little, Brown, 1913.

———. *Van Patten*. Boston: Little, Brown, 1926.

———. *The Voice at Johnnywater*. Boston: Little, Brown, 1923.

———. *White Wolves*. Boston: Little, Brown, 1927.

———. *The Whoop-Up Trail*. Boston: Little, Brown, 1933.

———. *The Wind Blows West*. Boston: Little, Brown, 1938.

British Columbia Assembly of First Nations. "Shíshálh." First Nations in BC. Accessed November 24, 2022. https://www.bcafn.ca/first-nations-bc/lower-mainland-southwest/shishalh.

Brown, Dee. *Bury My Heart at Wounded Knee: An Indian History of the American West*. New York: Henry Holt and Company, 1970.

California, County Marriages, 1850–1952. FamilySearch. 2022. https://www.familysearch.org/.

Canadian Traveller. "Pender Harbour: British Columbia's 'Venice of the North.'" *Canadian Traveller*, May 16, 2017. https://www.canadiantraveller.com/Pender-Harbour-British-Columbias-Venice-of-the-North.

Carlisle Indian School Digital Resource Center (searchable database). Carlisle PA: Dickinson College, ongoing. https://carlisleindian.dickinson.edu/student_files/robert-depoe-student-information-card.

Christian Science Board of Directors. "How Can I Be Healed?" Accessed November 24, 2022. https://www.christianscience.com/christian-healing-today/how-can-i-be-healed.

Confederated Tribes of Siletz Indians. "Changing Federal Policy & Reduction of the Coast Reservation by Act of Congress, 1875." Accessed December 1, 2022. https://www.ctsi.nsn.us/changing-federal-policy-reduction-of-the-coast-reservation-by-act-of-congress-1875/.

Dobie, J. Frank. *Coronado's Children*. Dallas: Southwest Press, 1930.

Dyer, Thomas G. *Theodore Roosevelt and the Idea of Race*. Baton Rouge: Louisiana State University Press, 1980.

Engen, Orrin A. *Writer of the Plains: A Biography of B. M. Bower*. Culver City CA: Pontine, 1973.

Furdell, William J. "Great Falls, Montana." In *Encyclopedia of the Great Plains*, edited by David J. Wishart, 169–70. 2nd ed. Lincoln: University of Nebraska Press, 2021. http://hdl.handle.net/2027/uva.x004903876.

Graham, Patricia Albjerg. *Community and Class in American Education, 1865–1918*. New York: Wiley, 1974.

Hallett, Hilary A. *Go West, Young Women! The Rise of Early Hollywood*. Berkeley: University of California Press, 2013.

Heaton, John W. *The Shoshone-Bannocks: Culture & Commerce at Fort Hall, 1870–1940*. Lawrence: University Press of Kansas, 2005.

Hinnant, Amanda, and Berkley Hudson. "The Magazine Revolution, 1880–1920." In *The Oxford History of Popular Print Culture: Volume Six: US Popular Print Culture 1860–1920*, edited by Christine Bold. New York: Oxford University Press, 2011. https://doi.org/10.1093/acprof:osobl/9780199234066.003.0007.

Hoosier State Chronicles. "Terre Haute Timeline." Vigo County Public Library, July 22, 2013. https://www.vigo.lib.in.us/spc/timeline/subject/historical.

Jou, Chin. "Counting Calories." Science History Institute, April 8, 2011. https://www.sciencehistory.org/distillations/counting-calories.

Keller, Betty. *Pender Harbour Cowboy: The Many Lives of Bertrand Sinclair*. Nanoose Bay BC: Heritage House, 2000.

Laegreid, Renée. "All-Girl Rodeo." In *Encyclopedia of Women in the American West*, edited by Gordon Moris Bakken and Brenda Farrington, 4–10. Thousand Oaks CA: Sage Publications, 2003.

Lamont, Victoria. *Westerns: A Women's History*. Lincoln: University of Nebraska Press, 2016.

Lovern, Blanche. Letter to the editor. *Frontier Times* 33, no.1 (Winter 1958–59): 38–39.

MacRae, Henry, director. *King of the Rodeo*. Starring Hoot Gibson. Screenplay by B. M. Bower. Universal Pictures, 1929. http://archive.org/details/Httparchive.orgkingoftherodeo.

Merchant, Peter. "As Far as the Eye Can See: The Shíshálh in Their Territory, 1791–1920." PhD thesis, University of British Columbia, 2020. https://doi.org/10.14288/1.0390350.

Minnesota, U.S., Death Index, 1908–2017. Ancestry. 1997–2022. https://www.ancestry.com/.

The Modernist Journals Project (searchable database). "Smart Set: 1910–1922." Brown and Tulsa Universities, ongoing. https://modjourn.org/journal/smart-set/.

Montana, County Marriages, 1865–1950. FamilySearch. 2022. https://www.familysearch.org/ark:/61903/1:1:f37w-nyd.

Montana Department of Public Instruction. *Biennial Report of the Superintendent of Public Instruction of the State of Montana*. Helena MT: Independent Publishing Company, 1894. http://archive.org/details/annualreportofau00mont.

Moore, Jacqueline M. *Cow Boys and Cattle Men: Class and Masculinities on the Texas Frontier, 1865–1900.* New York: New York University Press, 2010.

Native Land Digital. *Native Land.* 2022. https://native-land.ca/.

"News and Comment." *Oregon Historical Quarterly* 37, no. 4 (December 1936): 364–67.

New York, County Marriages, 1847–1848, 1908–1936. FamilySearch. 2022. https://www.familysearch.org/en/.

Oregon, U.S., State Divorces, 1925–1968. Ancestry, 1996–2022. https://www.ancestry.com/.

Oregon, U.S., State Marriages, 1906–1968. Ancestry, 1996–2022. https://www.ancestry.com/.

Pauly, Thomas H. *Zane Grey: His Life, His Adventures, His Women.* Urbana: University of Illinois Press, 2005.

Payne, Darwin. *Owen Wister, Chronicler of the West, Gentleman of the East.* Dallas: Southern Methodist University Press, 1985.

Peterson, Larry Len. *Charles M. Russell: Printed Rarities from Private Collections.* Missoula MT: Mountain Press, 2008.

Pollack, Alan. "Timeline of the Disaster." St. Francis Dam National Memorial Foundation. March 13, 2014. https://stfrancisdammemorial.org/timeline-of-the-st-francis-dam-disaster-and-los-angeles-aqueduct/.

Riley, Glenda. *Building and Breaking Families in the American West.* Albuquerque: University of New Mexico Press, 1996.

Schwartz, E. A. *The Rogue River Indian War and Its Aftermath, 1850–1980.* Norman: University of Oklahoma Press, 1997.

Sierra Madre's Wistaria Fete. Los Angeles Public Library Photo Collection. Calisphere. Accessed November 25, 2022. https://calisphere.org/item/f4f3f69fe86a823c6eed1572501a175c/.

Slide, Anthony. *Early American Cinema.* Metuchen NJ: Scarecrow Press, 1994.

Smith, Georgia Clarkson. "The Popular Magazine." Pulp Magazines Project. 2010. https://www.pulpmags.org/content/info/popular-magazine.html.

Smith, Helena Huntington. *The War on Powder River.* Lincoln: University of Nebraska Press, 1967.

Stiles, Anne. "Go Rest, Young Man." American Psychological Association. January 2012. https://www.apa.org/monitor/2012/01/go-rest.

Stephensen-Payne, Phil. "The Western and Frontier Fiction Magazine Index." Accessed May 9, 2023. http://www.philsp.com/homeville/wfi/0start.html.

United States Census, 1900, 1910, 1920, 1930, 1940. FamilySearch. 2022. https://www.familysearch.org/.

"Voter Information Guide for 1928, General Election." *Propositions*. Sacramento: California State Printing Office, January 1, 1928. https://repository.uchastings .edu/ca_ballot_props/251.

Wallis, Suzanne Fitzgerald, Sam Joyner, and Michael Wallis. *Art Deco Tulsa*. Charleston SC: History Press, 2018.

Washington, U.S., Marriage Records, 1854–2013. Ancestry, 1997–2022. https:// www.ancestry.com/.

Wilkins, Benjamin Ogden. "Charles Agnew McLean—Editor of the Popular Magazine." *Pulp Flakes*. May 16, 2015. http://pulpflakes.blogspot.ca/2015 /05/charles-agnew-mclean-editor-of-popular.html.

Williamson, Samuel H. "Seven Ways to Compute the Relative Value of a U.S. Dollar Amount, 1790 to Present." Measuring Worth, 2023. https://www .measuringworth.com/calculators/uscompare/.

INDEX

book rights, 61, 63, 66, 68–69,
  73, 81, 91, 93, 112
books in the early twen-
  tieth century, 25
Boston Globe, 43
Bower, Bella L. (née Belding), 139–41
Bower, Bertha Grace (daugh-
  ter), 6, 21–22, 82
Bower, Bertha Muzzy (B. M.):
  affiliation of with the I AM
  movement, 144–45; and arrival
  of Bud Cowan, 64–68; beginnings of as a writer, 10–14; and
  the Belmont Country Club,
  108–12; biography of, 35–36,
  58, 89, 144, 147–49; in Bliss
  ID (1911), 37–41; and bouts of
  depression, 92; and brother
  Chip Bower's wedding, 139–40;
  businesslike approach of, 10–11;
  and the Chicago rodeo, 98–101;
  and choice to leave children,
  21–22; and Christian Science,
  64, 80–81, 107, 131; and community engagement, 133–35; death
  of, 145–46; and death of son
  Roy Bower, 135–39; in Depoe
  Bay OR (1931), 121–40; diary of,
  89–97, 100–101, 103–4, 106–7,
  110–11, 116–17, 148; and Edmund
  Richard "Hoot" Gibson, 106–
  11, 113–14; and El Picacho
  Mine, 67–88, 108–10; on the
  Emma Alexander, 95–96; and
  estrangement from son Harry,
  82–83; and film projects, 66, 69,
  105–14, 117–18; Flying U ranch

stories, 15–20, 24, 44, 47, 99, 110,
  113, 131–32, 143; in Great Falls
  MT (1900–1907), 1–22, 23–29;
  Hollywood phase of, 47–54; and
  humor, 125; income and financial situation of, 12, 16, 20, 30,
  37, 41, 45, 54–57, 63, 66, 69, 73,
  80–81, 87, 88, 91–93, 104–7, 110–
  12, 116–20, 122–25, 131, 142; and
  King of the Rodeo (film), 111–15;
  in Las Vegas NV (1924), 83–87;
  later career of, 142–43; legacy
  of, 147–48; in Long Beach CA,
  104; in Los Angeles (1914–15),
  48–52; in Los Angeles (1919),
  63–68; in Los Angeles (1929),
  116–17; in Los Angeles (1938),
  140–42; and male-dominated
  spaces and sexism, 52, 60, 64,
  114–15; and marriage to Bill
  Sinclair, 23–36; and memoir of
  the Muzzy family's early years,
  143; and the mystery genre, 124–
  25; in Pender Harbor, British
  Columbia (1927), 95–98; and the
  Pocket ranch, 43–61; and publicity of identity, 26–27, 30, 39,
  42–43, 64, 73–76, 91–92, 112, 142,
  147; in Quincy CA (1913), 43–46;
  reworked material of, 132–
  33, 143; and road trips, 60–61,
  93–94, 133–34, 141; in San Francisco CA, 95–96; in San Jose CA
  (1912), 41–44; in Santa Cruz CA
  (1907), 29–32; in Sierra Madre
  CA (1926–27), 89–94; in Sierra
  Madre CA (1927–28), 103–16; at

the sms Ranch tx, 59–60; and
weight-loss and fitness, 107; and
women's organizations, 63–64,
74; and writing camps, 30–36, 82

Bower, Bertha Muzzy (B. M.), works
of: *The Adam Chasers*, 86–87,
89; "At the Grey Wolf's Den," 15;
"The Backsliding of Sister Stewart," 1, 12; *Cabin Fever*, 58; *Chip
of the Flying U*, 16–21, 24–26,
34, 41, 45–46, 47, 93, 106, 148;
Cow-Country, 67, 69, 77; *Dark
Horse*, 118–19, 123; *Desert Brew*,
72, 80; "The Dry Ridge Gang,"
32; *The Dry Ridge Gang*, 132;
Five Furies of Leaning Ladder,
133; *The Flying U Ranch*, 44;
The Flying U's Last Stand, 47,
51; *The Flying U Strikes*, 131–32;
Fool's Goal, 110–12, 115, 116; "The
Ghost in the Red Shirt," 12; *The
Gringos*, 42–45, 73–74; "Guileful Peppagee Jim," 26; "The
Hall of Mirth," 24; *The Haunted
Hills*, 132; *Hay-Wire*, 91, 94–95,
103–4, 109, 110; *The Heritage
of the Sioux*, 53–57; *Jean of the
Lazy A*, 51–52, 56–57; *Laugh-
ing Water*, 118; *Lonesome Land*,
9–11, 20–21, 24, 34–35, 39–41;
"The Long, Long Lane," 24; *The
Long Loop*, 117, 119; *The Look-
out Man*, 58; "The Maid and the
Money," 13, 26; *Man on Horse-
back*, 145; *Meadowlark Basin*,
84, 86, 110; *The North Wind Do
Blow*, 133, 139–40; *The Parowan
Bonanza*, 71, 77–81, 108; *The
Phantom Herd*, 52–54; *Pirates
of the Range*, 137; "The Place of
Sacrifice," 85–86; *Points West*,
89, 103, 108–9; *The Ranch at the
Wolverine*, 45, 54, 69; *Rim o' the
World*, 66; *Rocking Arrow*, 122–
25; *Rodeo*, 99, 104–6; *Shadow
Mountain*, 133; *The Singing Hill*,
142; *Skyrider*, 65; *Starr, of the
Desert*, 56–58; "The Strike of
the Dishpan Brigade," 5; *The
Swallowfork Bulls*, 91, 93; *Sweet
Grass*, 143; "That Other Coun-
try," 118; *The Thunder Bird*,
65; *Tiger Eye*, 117; *Trails Meet*,
124–25; *The Trollers*, 134–35;
Trouble Rides the Wind, 132;
The Uphill Climb, 38, 42; *Van
Patten*, 86; *The Voice at Johnny-
water*, 77; "When the Salt Has
Lost Its Savor," 12; *The White
Wolf Pack*, 87; *White Wolves*,
86–87; *The Whoop-Up Trail*, 131;
"Why Weary Went A-wooing,"
16; *The Wind Blows West*, 140

Bower, Billy (grandson), 133, 145
Bower, Bobby (grandson), 126
Bower, Cara Lou (grand-
daughter), 126, 137, 139
Bower, Cecelia (grand-
daughter), 137, 139
Bower, Clayton (first husband),
1, 5–11, 14–16, 20–21, 33,
34, 64, 124, 134, 145
Bower, Daisy (Harry's
wife), 126–27, 133
Bower, Dorothy (Harry's first
wife), 93–94, 105, 108

and *Lonesome Land*, 39–41; and
Meadowlark Basin, 84; new
book contract with, 66–70; as
new book publisher, 38–39; and
new Montana series, 81–82; and
The North Wind Do Blow, 133;
and *Pirates of the Range*, 137;
and the postwar years, 63; and
publicity of B. M. Bower's identity, 42–43, 64, 73–76, 91–92,
142; and *Rocking Arrow*, 123–24;
and *Rodeo*, 105–6, 114; shifts
in dealings with, 87; and *The
Swallowfork Bulls*, 91; and terms
of contract, 44–45; and "That
Other Country," 118; and *The
Trollers*, 135; and *Van Patten*, 86;
and *The Whoop-Up Trail*, 131;
and *The Wind Blows West*, 140
Livermore Sanitarium, 97
Lockhart, Caroline, 26, 75
Lonesome Land (Bower), 9–11,
20–21, 24, 34–35, 39–41
"The Long, Long Lane" (Bower), 24
Long Beach CA, 104
The Long Loop (Bower), 117, 119
The Lookout Man (Bower), 58
Los Angeles CA, 40, 48–52, 60–61,
63–68, 74, 110, 111, 116–17,
136–37, 140–42, 144–45
Los Angeles Times, 74, 109, 146
Los Gatos CA, 47, 51
lost mines in the desert, 67–68
Lovern, Blanche, 49, 56–58, 148
Lovern, Harry, 49

MacLean, Charles, 15, 20, 21,
26–27, 39, 42, 46, 56–57,
69, 91, 103, 111–12, 147

magazine fiction market, 1–2, 9,
11–13, 23–24, 26–27, 72–73,
87, 91, 115, 117, 142. *See also*
serial publications
"The Maid and the Money"
(Bower), 13, 26
male-dominated spaces and
sexism, 52, 60, 64, 114–15
Mankato, 2
Man on Horseback (Bower), 145
manuscript record books,
11, 35, 42, 133
manuscript records, 65, 138, 148
masculinity, 19–20, 43
Mattingly, Joe, 61
Maule, Harry, 91, 93, 95, 100, 115–16
McClure's Magazine, 1, 12, 51
McIntyre, Alfred, 57, 59–60, 63, 66,
70, 72–79, 87, 117–20, 123, 132
McLaughlin, Gene, 136–38
McNamara and Marlow,
1, 6, 11, 13, 14, 64
McWilliams, Eugene, 136–38
McWilliams, Walter, 136–38
Meadowlark Basin (Bower),
84, 86, 110
memoir of the Muzzy fami-
ly's early years, 143
mental health, 92
Mexican-American War, 42
Mexican territory, 42
Mike (woman from diary),
90, 105, 109
Miner, Lydia. *See* Benson, Lydia
(née Miner) (cousin)
Miner, Marcus Alonzo, 29, 36, 37, 40
Miner, Ruth, 36
Minnesota, 2, 5, 98

Printed in the USA
CPSIA information can be obtained
at www.ICGtesting.com
CBHW020227210524
8864CB00002B/83